*T*his book
belongs to

_____

...*a woman who desires
to experience God's
remarkable power
in her life.*

The Remarkable Women of the Bible

Elizabeth George

HARVEST HOUSE™ PUBLISHERS

EUGENE, OREGON

Cover by Terry Dugan Design, Minneapolis, Minnesota

Cover photo © IT Int'l/eStock Photography/PictureQuest

WOMAN AFTER GOD'S OWN HEART is a series trademark of The Hawkins Children's LLC. Harvest House Publishers, Inc., is the exclusive licensee of the federally registered trademark WOMAN AFTER GOD'S OWN HEART.

Acknowledgments

As always, thank you to my dear husband, Jim George, M.Div., Th.M., for your able assistance, guidance, suggestions, and loving encouragement on this project.

THE REMARKABLE WOMEN OF THE BIBLE
Copyright © 2003 by Elizabeth George
Published by Harvest House Publishers
Eugene, Oregon 97402
www.harvesthousepublishers.com

Library of Congress Cataloging-in-Publication Data
George, Elizabeth, 1944–
    The remarkable women of the Bible / Elizabeth George.
        p. cm.
Includes bibliographical references.
    ISBN 0-7369-0738-6 (pbk.)
    1. Women in the Bible. I. Title.
BS575.G464 2003
220.9'2'082—dc21
                                                                            2003012251

Printed in the United States of America.

05   06   07   08   09   10   11   12   / BP-KB /   13   12   11   10   9   8   7   6   5

Contents

An Invitation to...
a Remarkable Life

Remarkable! What a wonderful word to describe the women of the Bible! And, dear woman of faith, they—and their life-changing messages—are available to you and me today.

If you are like me, your life resembles one long obstacle course. Every day is filled with challenges. In spite of our schedules, plans, dreams, and goals, life keeps coming at us with its constant barrage of stress, problems, set-backs, and seemingly impossible situations. Truly, life can often seem to be more than we can manage on our own!

But, dear one, help—and hope—is available from the remarkable women of the Bible. You see, whatever we are dealing with, they have experienced it. They have met—and handled—the challenges of singleness, married life, and child-raising. They know about going without, about loss, about old age, about death and dying. All of the pain, the sorrow, the confusion, and the difficulties under the sun have touched their hearts. And now they live on in God's Word to instruct and encourage us as we cope with our lives today.

I like to think of each visit with these remarkable women as sitting down and having a cup of coffee with them. There they sit, in all their wisdom, ready, willing, and able to pass on what they have learned. They are more than happy to tell us how, through strong faith in God, they triumphed in their situations. Their hearts are open to you and me, and through their lives we can find great wisdom and practical help. And God has given us their lives in His Word so we can learn their life-changing messages!

Beloved, these dear women are God's gift to you and me. Whether or not you have a mother or a friend or a mentor who is available, you have the remarkable women of the Bible. Let them share with you. Let them encourage you. Let them counsel you. Let them show you the best way—God's way—to handle every day and every difficulty.

I also invite you to take advantage of the *Remarkable Women of the Bible Growth and Study Guide.* This helpful volume will propel you down the path toward living your own remarkable life by spurring you on as you seek to make the life-changing messages and timeless wisdom of God's corps of women of faith an integral part of your every day. The practical exercises contained in this growth and study guide are suitable for individual or group study and are for women of all ages whether married or single.

May God richly bless you as you look to Him and the remarkable women in His Word for His timeless principles for living your life today!

Eve

~

Remarkable Creation

Fairest of All Creation!

"Eve...was the mother of all living."
GENESIS 3:20
~

I wonder if there's a person on the face of the earth who hasn't heard of Adam and Eve, the first two people on the face of the earth? It seems that even a preschooler's education begins with the remarkable story of Adam and Eve.

As the first woman in the world, Eve enjoyed many firsts. And, as you'll soon see, it's not easy being first!

First Woman

God's first words about the creation of mankind are these: "So God created man in His own image; in the image of God He created him; male and female He created them" (Genesis 1:27). We can't help but wonder, How did it happen? Here's a short version of the creation of the "fairest creation of all," Eve!

Creation was complete. (Well, almost!) God had been busy for six days creating His beautiful new world. Now the stage was set. God's magnificent scenery stood finished and in place. His sun, moon, and stars lighted up His perfect planet. All creatures great and small enjoyed a perfect environment.

Yet all the universe stood at attention, awaiting God's final creations. At last God presented His masterpieces to the rest of nature. First the man Adam, formed by God from the dust of the ground (Genesis 2:7). Then—finally and dramatically—the woman Eve, made from one of Adam's ribs and presented by God to Adam as bone of his bones and flesh of his flesh (verses 21-22).

For now let's focus on the fact that God created Eve, deemed by poet laureate John Milton as the "fairest of creation." Devised by a perfect God, Eve reflected His divine perfection in her femaleness.

What can you do to join with Eve and revel in your lovely womanhood and femaleness?

Accept your remarkable femininity—There's no need to feel inferior, second-class, or second-rate. No, woman was God's last, most beautiful creation. It was only after God presented woman that He proclaimed His creation was "very good" (Genesis 1:31). Adam and Eve were alike, yet they were different from one another. One was male and one female (Genesis 1:27), yet together as well as individually they reflected God's image and His glory. Remarkable!

Begin to cultivate your remarkable femininity—This entire book is about the lovely, gracious, glorious, beautiful, prized-by-God women of the Bible. As you read along, allow God's truth to permeate your understanding and transform your view of yourself as a woman until it matches the high value God places on His women.

Commit to excelling in your remarkable role as a woman— As God's woman, be the best of the best (see Proverbs 31:29)! Delight in God's perfect design and plan for your life. He created you as a woman! As such, you join Eve's exalted position of "fairest of creation."

First Wife

Eve had the dual distinction of being the first-ever woman *and* the first-ever wife! Catch the scene: As God surveyed His creation on that historic sixth day, He noticed that there was no helper to complement the man, Adam. Up until this point, God had noted that "it was good" with each added day of creation. But in the case of Adam, God said, "It is *not* good that man should be alone; I will make him a helper comparable to him" (Genesis 2:18).

Eve, my new reading friend, was God's answer to Adam's incompleteness. Eve's number one role—and the purpose for her creation—was to complement Adam and to be a helper to her husband—to be a wife. This means Eve was created for a position of honor, being born to life's loveliest, most lofty throne of glory: "the glory of man" (1 Corinthians 11:7). The first wife reflected the glory of the first husband.

First to Fail

So far so good...until the perfect world that God created was thrown into sin and chaos by Eve's inability to withstand the temptations offered up by the serpent (Genesis 3:1-6). She listened to the tempter, ate of the one tree God had forbidden both her and Adam to eat from, involved her husband in rebellion...and the rest is history! This scene is now referred to as "the Fall."

What to do? "I know," Eve might have reasoned, "I'll blame the serpent!" (Genesis 3:13). But there was no doubt about her guilt. And there was no end to the changes that would take place...in her marriage...in her garden home...in her relationship with the Lord God Himself...and in her heart...due to her failure to obey God's instructions.

Then, just as darkness settled in on her wonderful and perfect life, she heard Adam declare, "Your name shall be called 'Eve, the mother of all living'" (see Genesis 3:20). With those words, Eve glimpsed a fresh ray of light—a future and a hope. She was Eve—the mother of all life!

Having been given a name filled with promise, Eve realized that she, the guilty sinner, could still serve her gracious and forgiving God. How? By bearing Adam's children and thereby becoming the mother of all generations (1 Corinthians 11:12). Her new name reflected the remarkable role she would have in the history of mankind.

"Eve." From death sprang life; from darkness, light; from an end, a beginning; from the curse, a blessing; from her sentence to death, a hope for the future; from the stinging despair of defeat, the strength of a budding faith. Eve was the mother of all living!

Do you realize that your life, dear one, counts, too? And counts significantly? True, you share Eve's sentence of physical death (Romans 5:12), but whoever you are and whatever your circumstances, you have life to give to and pass on to other people. How?

- You give life through your physical efforts to care for others.

- You share spiritual life by telling others about Jesus.

- You are the life of your home, bringing the sparkle of laughter and joy to other people.

- You pass physical life on to your children.

- You can also pass eternal life on to your children by teaching them the gospel of Jesus Christ.

So you, dear woman and remarkable creation, can choose daily to feed your spiritual life by sending your roots down deep into God's love and forgiveness. Eve's life came from the Lord, and so does yours. The Lord was the strength of her life, and He is your strength as well. All the energy of life, the purpose of life, all that you have of life to pass on finds its source in the Lord.

First Mother

My dear friend (and editor) Steve just coauthored a book entitled *Survival Guide for New Dads*.[1] Unfortunately, no such guide had been written for new moms when Eve became the first-ever mother. Why? Because it had never been done before! Never before had a woman given birth to a child. In fact, there had never before been a child—a baby (whatever *that* was!). Never before had the earth welcomed a baby.

What would you do with no mother or older woman to coach and encourage you? With a husband who hadn't been through childbirth preparation classes? With no girlfriends, textbooks, doctors, or nurses? With your first experience with physical pain? (That's right...before Eve's sin and the fall of mankind, there had been no pain.) Where would or could you turn for help?

That was Eve's dilemma. But she realized there was Someone she could turn to. And that Someone was all that she needed. She had the Lord. She could lean on Him no matter what new challenges her life might bring.

When her newborn babe arrived, Eve declared, "I have gotten a manchild with the help of the LORD" (Genesis 4:1 NASB). Eve knew that she had given birth to a baby—the first baby ever born—by the help of the Lord. And she knew that He—the Lord—was all she had needed. How grateful Eve must have been in this (yet another!) first venture to have the ever-present help of the Lord.

Eve was thankful, and you can be thankful, too—thankful that you can trust God for what has gone before, for what you are facing in the present, and for whatever happens in the future. Truly, He is all that you need!

Yes, Eve needed the Lord God to become the first-ever mother...and she was going to need Him again! Never could

Eve have guessed that Cain, the precious baby she held in her arms, would one day grow up to commit the first-ever crime and murder her second son, Abel, who became the first-ever human death. And little did she know that God would remove Cain, too, from her life. Not only did Eve experience many firsts, but she, along with Adam, was the first to experience loss.

First Lessons in Faith

Loss tears at the heart, and Eve certainly suffered many losses. Just look at the list. She had lost...

- her perfect relationship with God (Genesis 3:8)

- the bliss of a sinless marriage (Genesis 3:12)

- her lack of acquaintance with evil (Genesis 3:22)

- her ideal home in the Garden of Eden (Genesis 3:23)

- her son Abel, murdered by his brother (Genesis 4:8)

- her son Cain, whom God sent away (Genesis 4:14)

Yes, Eve had little left to lose and not much to hope for. She had dipped into her barrel of hope more times than she could count. She seemed to have no hope left, which, in itself, was another loss. It's been said that man can live—

> 40 days without food,
> three days without water,
> eight minutes without air...but
> only one second without hope.

But, oh, the goodness of the Lord! "Adam knew his wife again, and she bore a son and named him Seth, 'For God has appointed another seed for me'" (Genesis 4:25). The gift of Seth, whose name means *appointed*, surely refilled Eve's empty heart and her equally empty barrel of hope. "Appointed" by God, her Seth would bring not only hope to her sore heart, but he would be the one from whom God's Son would come, bringing bountiful and eternal hope to all mankind (see Luke 3:38).

Beloved, this Son—the Son of God—brings hope to you, too—even in seemingly absolute hopelessness. In Him there is help for every hurting heart…including yours.

How do you usually handle your heartbreaking losses? Rather than plunge into depression, discouragement, or hopelessness, place your God-given faith and confidence in these hope-filled realities:

> *God's faithfulness*—" 'For I know the plans I have for you,' declares the LORD, 'plans to prosper you and not to harm you, plans to give you hope and a future' " (Jeremiah 29:11 NIV).

> *God's promises*—One of the over 8000 promises in the Bible[2] assures you that you can do all things through Christ who strengthens you (Philippians 4:13).

> *God's goodness*—Your lack of hope can never negate God's goodness. Although weeping may endure for a night, because "the LORD is good; His mercy is everlasting, and His truth endures to all generations" (Psalm 100:5), "joy comes in the morning" (Psalm 30:5).

∼ *Eve's Message for Your Life Today* ∼

My mind is reeling as I am trying to take in the many wonderful truths the life of Eve, the first woman, sends to us across the pages of biblical history. For instance, do you realize that…

…you are created in the image of God? When God created woman, He created her in His image. Let it sink into your heart and mind that you are creative, intelligent, and rational. In these ways you are created in God's image.

...you are created to have fellowship and communion with God? No other creature has been granted the privilege of communing with God except man—the creature made most like Him.

...you are a reflection of God's glory? That's what being created in His image means. You reflect Him to other people. Every time you reach out in love, perform a deed of kindness, soften your heart in forgiveness, show a little extra patience, and follow through in faithfulness, other people experience the character of God through you! As a reflection of God's glory, why not:

Resolve never to worry about "self"-worth, but instead

Rejoice in your worth in God and your likeness to Him.

Resolve never to criticize or downgrade yourself, but instead

Rejoice that you are fearfully and wonderfully made (Psalm 139:14).

Resolve to seek a deeper relationship with God and to

Rejoice that He is near to all who call upon Him (Psalm 145:18).

Resolve to walk by faith paths you may not understand and to

Rejoice in the promise of His nearness as He directs your way.

Resolve to live each day as a child of God through His Son, Jesus Christ, and to be a reflection of His glory, and

Rejoice that, as one of God's chosen, your name is written in heaven (Luke 10:20)!

Resolve to spend time communing with God on a daily basis through prayer and the study of His Word, and

Rejoice in the strength He gives for each day and the hope He offers for all your tomorrows!

Resolve to reflect His glory and, dear one,

Rejoice in His love.

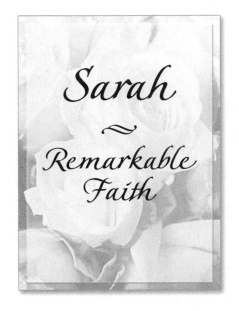

Sarah

~

Remarkable Faith

First Steps in Faith

"Abram took Sarai his wife...to the land of Canaan."
GENESIS 12:5

∼

aith—what a price tag it has! The life of faith is not an easy one. And that's exactly what Sarah,* our next remarkable woman of the Bible, discovered. Life was going quite well for her in her hometown of Ur. True, she and her husband, Abraham, didn't have any children yet (Genesis 11:30), but that may have been more bearable as long as she was surrounded by friends, family, and the distractions of the sophisticated and prosperous city of Ur, located on the lush banks of the Euphrates River. Like any other woman, Sarah must have loved home!

Leaving and Cleaving

But then Sarah was asked to leave behind all that was familiar and secure—to turn her back on all that she knew and go somewhere else. You see, God told Abraham to leave, to get out of Ur. And where were they to go? "To a land that I will

---

* Sarai is renamed Sarah by God. For consistency, I'll use Sarah throughout.

show you," is what the Lord said (Genesis 12:1). No pre-planned itinerary offered here!

As it turned out, Abraham—and Sarah with him—followed after God for the rest of his life, "not knowing where he was going," searching "for the city which has foundations, whose builder and maker is God." Abraham "died in faith, not having received the promises" (Hebrews 11:8-13). His was a homeless family...and that family included Sarah!

And, as it turned out, Sarah's minuscule seed of faith budded on that red-letter day when "they went out...from Ur of the Chaldeans" (Genesis 11:31). Possibly with pain in her heart and tears in her eyes, Sarah acted on God's instructions regarding marriage: "Therefore shall a man *leave* his father and his mother, and shall *cleave* unto his wife: and they shall be one flesh" (Genesis 2:24 KJV). As always, obedience to God boiled down to a faith-issue. However it happened, our Sarah took an important step of faith, and that faith grew and ultimately earned her a place of honor in God's Hall of Faith (Hebrews 11).

Are you wondering and praying, "Dear God, how can I begin taking the heavenward steps Sarah took and develop even greater faith?" Try these important first steps in faith today:

- *Trust the faith of those who lead you*—Whom is God using in your life to show you the path to greater faith?

- *Turn away from the pleasures of this world*—"Do not love the world or the things in the world" (1 John 2:15).

- *Turn toward the unknown, the unseen, the eternal, with a heart of faith*—"For we walk by faith, not by sight" (2 Corinthians 5:7).

Facing Famine

There are many kinds of famine God's women face on their life journeys. And, as we'll see, Sarah faced a variety in her long life marked by remarkable faith. And here's one such famine—a literal one!

"Oh, the heartache! Will it ever go away?" Perhaps these words darkened Sarah's thoughts the day she followed her full-of-faith husband, Abraham, out of Ur (Genesis 11:31). Ur had been Sarah's home, her life, but God told Abraham to go to Canaan. Leaving Ur may have been bad, but going to the land of Canaan was worse.

What could have made it worse? First of all, Ur was beautifully situated along the rich and fertile Euphrates River. Canaan was so far away—600 miles!—from her beloved hometown. Abraham may as well call it Nowhere Land!

Then, just when Sarah was getting used to Nowhere Land, a terrible famine struck, and it was time to move on again, this time to Egypt—another 300 miles away! Oh, surely, if only she and Abraham were still back in Ur then everything would be all right!

Maybe Sarah had thoughts like these. We really don't know, but we do know that a backward gaze can be dangerous. It can impede and harm our progress in faith. So what can we do to continue to look forward and faithfully follow God when the circumstances of life seem to worsen, when we must face a famine of some kind?

> **F**ace forward—Real life happens in the present, and God's blessings happen there (and in the future), too.

> **A**ccept your circumstances—The circumstances of life are one primary way God works in you and works out His will for you. Therefore "do all things without complaining and disputing" (Philippians 2:14).

> **If** your circumstances find you in God's will, you will find God in all your circumstances.

Trust in the Lord—God will keep you in perfect peace when your mind is stayed on Him in full trust (Isaiah 26:3).

Hope for the future—Hope in God is always the bright star that lights your path in any present darkness...and on into the unknown future.

～ *A prayer to pray* ～

Dear God of "Sarai,"
grant that such a one as I
may see the good in bad
and the faith to be had...following Thee!

Facing Fear

Every year, women who desire greater beauty spend billions of dollars on makeup, hair treatments, dental work, cosmetic surgeries, and physical conditioning. There seems to be no price too high for beauty. Do you ever wish for greater beauty? Oddly, there were days when Sarah may have wished she were *less* beautiful!

God had blessed Sarah with great beauty—with *remarkable* beauty! At her birth her proud parents had appropriately named her Sarah, meaning "princess." But beauty isn't everything! Sometimes Sarah's beauty was a blessing...and other times it was a curse.

Genesis 12 tells about one of those cursed times. As Sarah traveled with her husband Abraham, their caravan ran up against the powerful Egyptian pharaoh. Although this impressive leader possessed massive military forces and great wealth, he wanted one more thing, the beautiful Sarah—our Sarah!—as an addition to his harem.

Amazingly, Sarah's husband had predicted this exact scene. (How had he known?) In fact, Abraham and Sarah had discussed such a possibility, and now it was reality (Genesis

12:11-13). Abraham's solution to the potential problem? It went something like this: "Let's lie. We'll tell them you're my sister. Well, it's not really a lie. After all, even though you are my wife, you're also my father's daughter. You know—a half-sister, a half-lie? At least *my* life will be spared!"

What was Sarah to do with *her* fear?

There is "a time to keep silence" (Ecclesiastes 3:7). Write this wise principle upon the tablet of your heart for life's seasons of testing. Sarah learned this costly principle as she ran up against fear (more times than she cared to count!) on her journey toward greater faith.

Let's review. Sarah's journey began in obedience. Faithfully following her husband, as he faithfully followed God, she set out toward Canaan. Severe famine forced them south to the foreign land of Egypt. Fear for his life, mixed with fear of the famine, moved Abraham, the great patriarch of Israel, to lie to the powerful pharaoh about his exquisite wife. "She is my sister," Abraham said. So Sarah was taken to the pharaoh's house and into his harem.

Surely Sarah wondered with fear, "What will happen to me? Will Abraham go on without me? Will I ever see him again? What will life be like as a member of a harem?" We don't know, because Scripture is silent. But don't you hope the silence indicates Sarah's faith as she sat in her harem-prison, faced her fears, and waited on the Lord?

Strength for today and hope for tomorrow are sometimes realized—by you and me as well as by Sarah—in the silent patience of faith.

- ℘ Wait on the LORD; be of good courage, and He shall strengthen your heart (Psalm 27:14).

- ℘ Rest in the LORD, and wait patiently for Him (Psalm 37:7).

- ℘ Truly my soul silently waits for God (Psalm 62:1).

> ❧ Those who wait on the LORD shall renew their strength (Isaiah 40:31).

> ❧ It is good that one should hope and wait quietly (Lamentations 3:26).

> ❧ Blessed is he who waits (Daniel 12:12).

Dear one, make it your practice to wait on the Lord, to trust in Him, to hope in Him...and to be blessed in your silence of faith.

Trusting in the Lord

Are you wondering how Sarah's predicament turned out? What happened next?

All I can say is that what happened next was *God*—God to the rescue! Yahweh, the God of Abraham and Sarah, was watching and waiting as the human drama of their journey toward greater faith unfolded. At the perfect moment, when things seemed blackest, Yahweh made His dramatic, miraculous appearance. Although He was never seen, His works were most certainly seen, heard, felt, and noted...and never forgotten! It was God to the rescue as "the LORD plagued the pharaoh and his house with great plagues because of Sarai, [Abraham's] wife" (Genesis 12:17). Wow, what a scene! And what a rescue!

Now, dear reading friend, do you realize that the God of Sarah is also your God? With God all things are possible—even deliverance from the impossible and the unbearable (Matthew 19:26). Yahweh knows how to make a way of escape for His children (1 Corinthians 10:13). He, the Lord, is able to deliver thc godly out of trials (2 Peter 2:9). In His own time and in His own way, God rescues His people. So even when you feel awfully alone and your situation seems horribly hopeless, know that you are *never* alone and *never* without hope! "God is our refuge and strength, a very *present* help in trouble.

Therefore we will not fear" (Psalm 46:1-2). Therefore, dear one, you must trust in the Lord!

Trusting the Lord...Again and Again!

But hang on! We're not done with Sarah's story! Twenty-five years later, our remarkable Sarah was forced to hone her faith again in an almost identical second such harem experience. Indeed, the entire scene in Genesis 20 is almost a scene-by-scene, word-by-word, blow-by-blow repeat. Evidently once in such a fearful situation wasn't enough to grow a remarkably *beautiful* woman into a remarkably beautiful woman of remarkable *faith!*

Many lessons in faith require numerous review sessions. After all, trust in the Lord is like a multifaceted gem. A facet is cut, the gem turned, and another facet incised. So, in a repeat trial, God once again turned Sarah's life in order to more clearly imprint the beauty of faith into her soul. Surely the chisel of trial hurt, just as it had 25 years before when Abraham first put her life—and their future—in jeopardy. She had ended up in the harem of an ungodly, heathen ruler...all because she was still—at age 90!—so remarkably beautiful. But God seemed to be asking Sarah to turn her face, her fears, and her faith once again toward Him and to, once again, trust Him.

After all, what had she learned those decades ago about trusting the Lord? Or, put another way, what are some of the great lessons in the making of great faith?

> ❧ *Lesson 1: Pray*—"The righteous cry out and the LORD hears, and delivers them out of all their troubles" (Psalm 34:17).

> ❧ *Lesson 2: Trust*—"Trust in the LORD with all your heart, and lean not on your own understanding"—or anyone else's (Proverbs 3:5)!

  ❧ *Lesson 3: Believe*—"Faith is the substance of things hoped for, the evidence of things not seen" (Hebrews 11:1).

  ❧ *Lesson 4: Wait*—"I waited patiently for the LORD; and He inclined to me, and heard my cry" (Psalm 40:1).

～ *Sarah's Message for Your Life Today* ～

Dear one, there's a loud, repeated message here from Sarah's life to yours. As you enter into *your* new day, is something in your life a "repeat" problem? Are there daily difficulties you constantly face? Are there people who regularly let you down or fail to follow through? Are there seemingly impossible hardships to be endured day after day?

Imagine the sheer beauty your faith will have as you allow God, time after time and day after day, to use life's difficulties and disappointments to lead you to deeper trust in Him. May the four chapters that follow—four lessons about first steps in living a life of faith drawn from Sarah's journey in the presence of God—encourage you to again and again lift your soul before the Author of your faith (Hebrews 12:2) and allow Him, again and again, to add to the exquisite gem of your faith yet additional sparkling facets.

As you trust in the Lord...again and again...remember that, just like Sarah, you live your life in God's constant and powerful presence. No matter where you are, no matter what you must leave behind, no matter where you are required to go or what you are asked to give up or to do without, no matter what odds you encounter, no matter how alone you feel or appear to be, no matter who has let you down or forsaken you, you are *never* alone, for...

  ❧ *Above you* are God's overshadowing wings (Psalm 91:4).

⚘ *Beneath you* are God's everlasting arms (Deuteronomy 33:27).

⚘ *Around you* the angel of the Lord encamps on all sides to deliver you (Psalm 34:7).

⚘ *Inside you* God's peace that passes all understanding guards your heart and mind (Philippians 4:7).

Advanced Steps in Faith

"Is anything too hard for the LORD?"
GENESIS 18:14

~

Proper etiquette teaches us that, when introducing two strangers to one another, we should try to share something about each person so the two new acquaintances will be able to carry on a conversation. When God introduced Sarah to the world, He used only eight words: "But Sarai was barren; she had no child" (Genesis 11:30).

Eight words. A simple statement of a cold, hard fact. Sarah had no child. These first words tell us volumes about Sarah, don't they?

Perhaps Sarah wondered, "What's gone wrong? What have I done? Why hasn't God blessed me with children?" On and on Sarah's questioning may have gone...and on and on went her pain. Nothing could relieve it, soothe it, take it away. Childlessness was a stigma in Sarah's day, and by all indications in the Bible, it was a stigma that seared itself more deeply into Sarah's soul with each childless sunrise.

What was Sarah's solution? What was her battle plan with each sad, bewildered, possibly even bitter thought? How did Sarah handle an ongoing problem?

Answer: For 25 years—*25 years!*—Sarah would have to reach, reach back on many occasions with the fingers of faith to clutch God's many promises of offspring. With aching heart and stinging tears, Sarah would have to trust God one more time, for one more day...day after day...for 25 years. She would have no other option. She would have to resist faithlessness, despite the great temptation to give up, succumb to bitterness, lash out at her husband, turn her back on God, or give in to the contentious spirit that hovered nearby as an easy option. Our beautiful Sarah would learn one thing, a lesson that sprang forth from a pain-filled soil:

～ Faith is the better way to face the distresses of life. ～

Reaching for God's Promises

Dear reader, you and I have the advantage of reading ahead in the Bible to find out how Sarah handled an ongoing problem. And as we fast-forward a bit into Sarah's story, please note that dealing with barrenness became the means for Sarah to graduate to "Advanced Steps in Faith."

Here now is the blueprint by which Sarah, the wife and traveling companion of Abraham and herself a follower of God, would build a life of greater—and great—faith. In a nutshell, Sarah would have to remember—and reach for—a promise that would profoundly affect her, a promise God would make to Abraham: "I will make you a great nation...to your descendants I will give this land" (Genesis 12:2,7).

Beloved, what do you do with a promise from God? You follow in Sarah's footsteps. You follow her remarkable example of faith. You reach for that promise for as long as you must—even for 25 years or more.

Twenty-five years. Think about it! For 25 years Sarah grabbed onto God's promise of an heir one more time, for one more day, until her son, Isaac, was finally born! Do you realize that those years add up to well over 9000 faith-reaches? So Sarah blesses you and me with her example. Her message to us is, whatever impossible, unbearable, unusual, unchangeable test awaits you this day (or for the next 8999 days, or *forever!*), by faith, we are to reach one more time for the "exceedingly great and precious promises" of God (2 Peter 1:4)! Yes, faith is the better way—indeed, the only way!—to face the distresses of life.

Continuing to Believe

At least five times God promised Abraham a son, a seed, off-spring (Genesis 12–17)—and still there was no son! And keep in mind that time is passing (we're at about the 25-year mark since Sarah first heard the promise). Keep in mind, too, that the beautiful Sarah is aging (she's now near 90!)...and still no son. True, for a while they thought Ishmael—Abraham's son born of their maidservant Hagar—was "the son of promise."

Yet now God was saying again to Abraham, "I will bless her and also give you a son by her....*Sarah* your wife shall bear you a son" (Genesis 17:16,19). As we noted, Sarah had heard the promise before, but this time there was a new twist: God spoke specifically of *her!* No wonder Abraham fell down and had a good laugh (Genesis 17:17). After all, Sarah was 90 years old and Abraham was himself a hundred!

Again God's promise seemed absurd! "How," Sarah may have wondered, "can one continue to believe God's promises when the situation seems impossible and the waiting endless?" Note these answers, dear one:

> *By choice*—The opposite of faith is disbelief—ugly, black doubt! When God presents you with one of His dazzling promises, He is offering you the choice of either

accepting its brilliance and being led by its light or smothering it in the dark cloud of your doubt.

By faith—Strength for today and hope for tomorrow are realized only as you put your faith in God's promises. Faith is "the evidence of things *not* seen" (Hebrews 11:1). We see God's answers and enjoy His strength and hope only through the eyes of faith.

By exercise—Your faith is like a muscle. It grows with exercise and, over time, increases in strength and size. Every time you choose to exercise your faith, you gain further strength for each day and greater hope for each tomorrow.

Which area of *your* life, dear woman of faith, calls for you to continue to believe and to choose to exercise your faith— by faith—today? Is it a physical problem like Sarah's was? A family problem? A personal struggle? A financial test? Does there seem to be no rhyme or reason to the circumstances, no end to the waiting in sight, no solution to the predicament? Choose to wield your faith one more time! Stretch it! Strain it! Grow it! Trust in God because "there has not failed one word of all His good promise" (1 Kings 8:56).

Continuing On

Can you believe it? We're still in fast-forward mode! We're continuing to learn about something that is *going* to happen but *hasn't* happened. That's how God chose to mold our Sarah's striking and strong faith, a faith that would place her in God's gallery of the greats of faith (Hebrews 11). As we know, God gave the beautiful-but-barren Sarah a beautiful promise of a child, a son. As you'll soon see, the promises kept piling up...and so did the years. And still no son!

And now here came another promise tumbling out of heaven as God communicated with Abraham concerning

Sarah—"She shall be a mother of nations" (Genesis 17:16). As if that weren't enough, God elaborated, extending the promise to the end of time—"She shall be a mother of nations; kings of peoples shall be from her." And beloved, it happened, just as God said it would! In time, Sarah's ancestors became "as the stars of the heaven and as the sand which is on the seashore" (Genesis 22:17). The roll call of Sarah's descendants includes the patriarchs of the faith, kings of nations, and the Savior of the world, Jesus Christ—right on down to *you* if you've been born spiritually into the line of Abraham through Christ (see Romans 4:16-25). The lowly Sarah, pilgrim from Ur and stranger in Canaan, became the progenitor of all the saints through all the ages!

Beloved, there is no way to measure the continuing influence of one godly mother. In 1703, a godly woman named Esther Edwards gave birth to a son she named Jonathan. From this woman's son, who would become distinguished as a theologian and preacher, came an amazing line of offspring. More than 400 have been traced, and that number includes 14 college presidents and 100 professors. Another 100 were ministers of the gospel, missionaries, and theological teachers. Still another 100-plus were lawyers and judges, 60 were doctors, and as many more were authors and editors of high rank. What a tribute to this godly and prayerful mother! As you can see, her godly influence continued on!

Sarah and Mrs. Edwards. And still there's another woman who can also become a mother of nations...and that woman is *you!* God's mandate to you is to faithfully teach your children the lifesaving, life-giving truths of Scripture, which can bring your children into God's family (2 Timothy 3:14-15). With Christ in *your* heart, you begin your own line of godly seed. As you pass on the gospel to your precious children, they can, in turn, pass it on to the next generation. Your godly influence can continue on through time and through generations as innumerable as the stars and the sand!

Are you thinking, "But I don't have children. This doesn't apply to me"? Oh, but it does! *You* can aid in the birth of spiritual children by sharing the truth about Jesus Christ. *You* can help bring many into the line of Christ. *You* can add fellow saints to God's great cloud of witnesses (Hebrews 12:1). And you can do so by speaking up at work, inviting your co-workers, neighbors, and family members to church, and sharing how Jesus has changed your life and given you His strength for today and His hope for tomorrow. You, too, can be a mother of nations!

Advancing in Faith

It's exciting to think and dream of a faith that affects the world, isn't it? But we mustn't forget the general principle that doing great things *for* God requires great faith *in* God. So... how does a woman advance in faith? How does such growth occur? What steps can a woman (especially women like you and me!) take to grow into the position of becoming a pillar of faith like our dear Sarah did?

Let's review the "Advanced Steps in Faith" we've learned so far from Sarah's life—

Continue to remember God's promises
...and reach for them.
Continue to believe God's promises
...and reach for them.
Continue to continue to remember
and believe God's promises
...and reach for them
...no matter what!

Answering a Question

And now let's learn from Sarah yet another lesson in faith that began with a question: "Is anything too hard for the LORD?" How you answer this question indicates the level of your faith in God. The angel of the Lord asked this question of Sarah, our great heroine of faith (Genesis 18:14). Only she wasn't exhibiting much faith at the time. Here's what happened.

First, there had been the promise. God promised a child, a seed, a son of Abraham to be born by Sarah. And Sarah had been hearing about that for 25 years! She had almost quit paying attention.

Then there were the facts. Sarah was 90 years old, well past the age of childbearing. Sarah was also well aware that she had "grown old" (literally, worn out, withered, ready to fall apart like an old garment). At this point, having a baby would take a miracle!

Next, there was the laugh. "Sarah laughed within herself" (Genesis 18:12). As she thought about the absurdity, the impossibility of giving birth, her laugh of doubt rang forth.

Then came the question—the same question God asks of you and your faith: "Is anything too hard for the LORD?" Literally, "Is any word from God too wonderful, too impossible, for Jehovah?" With divine omnipotence as a factor in the equation, the answer to that question resounds to the heavens and back: *"No!"* Nothing promised by God is ever beyond His resources, His ability, His love! *Nothing!*

So, dear one, with the flame of the faith you possess from God, search your heart for any dark corner of doubt about God's ability to accomplish all things for you.

    ♪ Is this day of your life too hard for the Lord?

    ♪ Is the physical difficulty you are bearing too hard for the Lord?

    ♪ Is the heartache you suffer too hard for the Lord?

    ♪ Is the problem in your marriage or family too hard for the Lord?

    ♪ Is your financial condition too hard for the Lord?

❦ Is the path you're on too hard for the Lord?

No! Nothing—I repeat, *nothing!*—you face is beyond the resources, the ability, or the love of your heavenly Father!

∿ *Sarah's Message for Your Life Today* ∿

Every woman of remarkable faith begins her trek with first steps in faith that soon accelerate to advanced steps in faith. And promotions in a life of faith—like those in school—don't come easily! Required courses must be continually completed before the diploma is beautifully scripted, signed, and sealed by the appropriate officials.

Genesis 17 offers God's snapshot of Sarah's hard-earned promotion in the school of faith. On that day God said, "As for Sarai...you shall not call her name Sarai, but Sarah shall be her name" (verse 15).

Exactly what courses had Sarah completed that qualified her for this promotion? As you read along, grade yourself in the blanks provided. Hear Sarah's message to your life and to your heart.

1. *Sarah had learned to follow her husband*—Sarah completed Faith 101 when she learned to trust and follow Abraham as he followed after God (Genesis 12:1). True, her life was one of radical moves and difficult change. But she accepted her lifestyle as God's will and her husband as God's instrument in her life. _____

2. *Sarah had learned to trust the Lord*—Sarah almost failed this course, but by God's grace her faith held up to the fingernail-scraping edge while she huddled alone with her fears—and faith—in the pharaoh's harem. Her own husband, her Abraham, had failed her. Would God fail her, too? She hoped... she prayed...she trusted He wouldn't (1 Peter 3:5-6). As she

walked out of her hostage situation, amazed at God's miraculous solution (Genesis 12:15-20), Sarah's score on this exam of faith soared. _____

3. *Sarah had learned to wait on God*—Actually, she was still learning to wait. Already enrolled in Faith 102, Sarah was getting the instruction she needed to continue in her 25-year wait on God's promise that she and Abraham would have a son. No, waiting was not—and never had been—easy for Sarah. _____

4. *Sarah had learned the importance of having a gentle and quiet spirit*—Yes, her name *Sarah* carried the connotation of "contention," as well as the meaning of "princess." (And she had certainly been contentious with her maid Hagar, another story in itself—see Genesis 16.) What a painful time of learning! How thankful she was to now be adorning herself regularly with the gentle and quiet spirit that pleases God (1 Peter 3:4-5). _____

Well, dear follower of God, how well did you score on this quiz? Consider what you can do to grow in these areas and make plans for progress. After all, many more classes come after Faith 101 and Faith 102 in this lifelong journey with the God you love.

Rewards of Faith

"And the LORD did for Sarah as He had promised."
GENESIS 21:1 (NASB)

〜

"They that wait on the Lord—"
Teach us to wait, we pray,
And prove the blessings from Thy Word
By waiting day by day.[1]

*T*here is no time lost in waiting...*if* you are waiting on the Lord. Sarah, the one God had called "a mother of nations" (Genesis 17:16), waited on the Lord for 25 years! Clutching God's remarkable promise for a son, she had waited—right on past her childbearing years. The future looked hopeless, and although she had her moments of doubt, yet she hoped—hoped on the words the Lord Himself had spoken: "At the appointed time...Sarah shall have a son" (Genesis 18:14).

Waiting on the Lord

"At the appointed time." These words call us to the discipline of waiting on God's timing, of waiting until His "appointed time." These words call us to a deeper faith because "to everything there is a season" (Ecclesiastes 3:1). And nothing is harder than waiting. Yet all of us wait for something. And in God's School of Waiting, He teaches and transforms us as we wait. For what do you wait? Savor these special blessings while you wait on God's "appointed time":

Blessing #1: Increased value—Waiting increases the value and importance of the thing waited for. Whether you're waiting for deliverance from suffering, the discovery of God's purposes, direction for your confused life, a home at last, a wedding day, a family reunion, a prodigal's return, or a child's birth, waiting makes the desired object a greater treasure once it is received.

Blessing #2: Increased time—No one has enough time. But the one who waits is given the precious gift of time—time to embrace life's circumstances, time to press closer to God's loving and understanding heart, time to grow in the hard-won grace of patience, time to feel more deeply the pain of others who also wait with flickering faith.

Blessing #3: Increased faith—The writer of Hebrews defines faith as "the substance of things hoped for, the evidence of things not seen" (Hebrews 11:1). Please read the rest of Hebrews 11, and notice how the saints through the ages (including Abraham and Sarah) had their faith increased by waiting. Faith grows and is strengthened through time.

So while you wait, dear one, be of good courage, and *He,* the One upon whom you wait, shall strengthen your heart *while* you wait (see Psalm 27:14).

Waiting on the Promises

We must not only learn to wait on the Lord and on His perfect timing, but we also wait on His promises. For Sarah and Abraham, the aged couple to whom God had for 25 years repeatedly promised a son, their time of waiting was finally over. Out of heaven the reward for the faith of this dear, literally "worn out" (as in the physical youth and vitality needed for procreation) couple arrived...*and the LORD did for Sarah as He had promised* (Genesis 21:1, NASB)! In the quiet precision of His ordained, from-before-the-foundation-of the-world control, God did for Sarah exactly as He had promised. Divine grace and miraculous power were at work in Sarah's once-lifeless womb, and a baby son was on the way—exactly as God had promised.

What has God promised you, one of His precious women? The Bible contains as many as 8000 promises. In difficulty and disaster, in trial, tragedy, trauma, and testing, in times of spiritual, emotional, and physical darkness, you can trust these promises. You can be assured that God will do for you, too, exactly as He has promised.

Another woman-of-faith, a young French woman, once created a "promise box" to teach her children that the promises of God bring special comfort in times of need. The small box contained 200 handwritten promises copied out of the Bible onto small pieces of paper. Little did she know that her own trust in the Lord would be severely tested in wartime France!

With no food available for her family—her children emaciated and hungry, wearing rags and shoes without soles—she turned to her promise box. In desperation she prayed, "Lord, O Lord, I have such great need. Is there a promise here that is really for me? Show me, O Lord, what promise I can have in this time of famine, nakedness, peril, and sword." Blinded by tears, she reached for the box to pull out a promise and knocked it over. God's promises showered down all around her, on her lap, and on the floor! Not one was left in the box. What supreme joy in the Lord she found as she realized that *all* of the promises of God were hers—in the very hour of her greatest need![2]

My dear friend, He who has promised is faithful (Hebrews 10:23). God will fulfill His promises. Your responsibility is to wait patiently and to believe His exceedingly great and precious promises and trust in the Promise Maker (2 Peter 1:4).

Waiting on a Miracle

If there had been a newspaper in their day, the reporter assigned to the story of Abraham and Sarah's life would have received some amazing answers to his basic journalistic questions.

Who?   Abraham, the 100-year-old-father, and Sarah, the 90-year-old mother, are proud parents of a baby boy (Genesis 17:17).

What?   With God's blessing, Sarah conceived and bore a son (Genesis 21:2).

When?   At the appointed time, God fulfilled His promise to the elderly couple (Genesis 18:14).

Why?   The miracle fulfilled what the "God, who cannot lie" had promised long ages before (Titus 1:2; Genesis 12:2).

How?   "By faith Sarah...received strength to conceive seed, and she bore a child when she was past the age, because she judged Him faithful who had promised" (Hebrews 11:11).

There is only one conclusion to be reached: *It was a miracle!* This miraculous birth occurred because God fulfilled a promise made 25 years prior to His two believing saints, Sarah and Abraham.

And it is no different for you, dear woman-of-faith. What has God promised to you, His believing saint? What do you, by faith, believe to be true of God? Note the "miracles":

　♪ *Eternal life*—"I give them eternal life" (John 10:28).

　♪ *Sufficient grace*—"My grace is sufficient" (2 Corinthians 12:9).

　♪ *Strength for life*—"I can do all things through Christ who strengthens me" (Philippians 4:13).

　♪ *His everlasting presence*—"The LORD your God is with you wherever you go" (Joshua 1:9).

Dearly beloved, these are but a few of the precious jewels of promise stored in God's Word (the Bible being yet another "miracle"). Open the Scriptures. Pour out its golden coins stamped with the image of heaven's King. Let the treasure flow through your fingers. Count the diamonds of promise that flash like stars. Marvel over the royal rubies of guarantee. Imagine the worth of each single gem of promise. This treasure of promises is God's inheritance for you. By faith know and cherish what the Faithful One has promised!

Waiting on the Reward

Waiting: "to remain inactive in readiness or expectation." This is how the dictionary defines what Sarah had just spent 25 years doing—waiting! Oh, how difficult it must have been for Sarah to remain inactive in readiness and expectation of God's promised son! But there is wealth in waiting! For Sarah the waiting meant precious treasure. The riches and the reward at the end of her wait included...

　♪ *The witnessing of miracles*—The 100-year-old Abraham fathered a child! The 90-year-old Sarah conceived and bore a son! And still another miracle followed as Sarah's worn-out body sustained the life of her little one as she nursed him.

♪ *The working of faith*—Sarah inherited the promise of a child by "faith and patience"; she exhibited the full assurance of hope until the end (Hebrews 6:11-12).

♪ *The fulfillment of God's promise*—Wrapped up in Sarah's little baby was God's fulfillment of His covenant with Abraham (Genesis 12:2), and the continuance of the family line that would give rise to God's own Son, Jesus Christ (Matthew 1:2,17).

♪ *A child to love*—God made the barren Sarah "a joyful mother of children" (Psalm 113:9).

For what are you waiting? For what are you remaining "inactive in readiness of expectation"? Are you waiting for a prodigal to return to his or her Father? Are you waiting for release from some physical affliction? Perhaps you are waiting for a husband—or for your husband to return to the Lord, or to love the Lord more deeply, or to be the spiritual leader in your home. Could it be you are waiting, like sister Sarah, for a baby? Or are you waiting for vindication from some unfortunate misunderstanding, for God to come to your rescue and show forth His righteousness on your behalf (Psalm 37:6)? Are you eagerly waiting for heaven, for the groaning of your body to cease, for your ultimate victory, to go home to the heavenly abode for which you so long?

God bids you to wait—in readiness and expectation—on His riches, on His reward, just as Sarah did, whose sister you are as you trust in God (1 Peter 3:5-6).

Waiting on Joy

The English Bible doesn't say it—but, oh, does the Hebrew language ever say it! The desert tent rang with sounds of *joy!* Sarah could not contain her gladness as she held her promised son. It was a season of joyous celebration. Sarah's shameful barrenness had ended. Finally—*finally!*—after 25 years, after hearing the promise again and again, after a visit from God and two angels (Genesis 18:1-2), little Isaac, new and wrinkled, was born to the aged and wrinkled—but laughing—parents, Abraham and Sarah. And in their exultant joy, they named the babe *Isaac,* meaning "he laughs."

Once again Sarah was laughing. Oh, she had laughed before when the angels and the Lord had again promised the child. But then her laughter had been rooted in disbelief (Genesis 18:12). Now she exulted, for, in her own words, "God has made me laugh" (Genesis 21:6). Now hers was the hearty laughter of joy upon joy! "Who would have dreamed?" Sarah probably marveled. Certainly not she! But God, who is always fully able, had accomplished the miracle. Others would no longer laugh at her—now they would laugh with her in joy.

This definitely was an occasion for joy. Isaac was Sarah's reward. He was the child of her own body, the child of her old age, the child of God's promise, the fruit of tested faith, the gift of God's grace, and the heaven-appointed heir. So Sarah sang a jubilant song of pure joy, the first-recorded cradle hymn of a mother's thankfulness and delight.

Dear woman of God, join with Sarah in this chorus of praise! Even if life is difficult *here,* you can know joy because of the hope you have in Christ. *Here* you have cause to sing even when you don't feel like singing, even when God's promises aren't yet fulfilled. At the appointed time—here or in heaven—God will give you reason to sing as He demonstrates His faithfulness to you. But sing now as you look forward to the fulfillment of all His promises to you and to your season of joy!

> Weeping may endure for a night, but *joy* comes in the morning....You [God] have turned for me my mourning into dancing; You have put off my sackcloth and clothed me with gladness (Psalm 30:5,11).

God will comfort all who mourn. He will "give them beauty for ashes, the oil of joy for mourning, the garment of praise for the spirit of heaviness" (Isaiah 61:2-3)—and that "all" includes you, dear faithful one! *Rejoice!*

∼ Sarah's Message for Your Life Today ∼

It's impossible to miss Sarah's message to our lives today, isn't it? It's all about faith—remarkable faith! The word *faith* describes Sarah's life in one word. And we cannot say goodbye to this "mother of us all" without slipping quietly into the hallowed halls of Hebrews 11, God's portrait gallery of great men- and women-of-faith who have loved Him through the ages. There we can't help but notice the larger-than-life pictures of Noah, Abraham, Isaac, Jacob, Joseph, Moses, and Joshua. But just as grand is the portrait of the gentle and quiet-spirited Sarah who possessed a strong-as-steel faith (see 1 Peter 3:1-6). Her faith shines as brightly as that of the other people listed on this holy roster!

What merited dear Sarah's inclusion in faith's Hall of Fame?

Motherhood—This blessing came late to the long-barren Sarah who, at age 90, finally bore Isaac! And once the blessing was bestowed, Sarah was a fierce, loyal mother to her precious son (see Genesis 21)! Underneath her portrait we read these words, put there by God Himself: "By faith Sarah herself also received strength to conceive seed, and she bore a child when she was past the age, because she judged Him faithful who had promised" (Hebrews 11:11).

Mother of a nation—Sarah has been esteemed throughout time as a kind of mother figure to God's chosen nation of Israel. From Sarah and her husband Abraham, and through their son Isaac, come—through faith—all true believers, God's chosen people through time (Romans 4:16).

Mother of faith—Hebrews 11 points to the acts of faith of those who preceded us in time, and Sarah is the first woman named. And once again, what was her outstanding act of faith? The answer once again is this: Sarah considered God faithful and able to follow through on His promise of a son in her old age.

Dear one, "with God nothing will be impossible" (Luke 1:37). Nothing is too hard for the Lord! So I ask you, what trials and temptations do you currently face? Does some difficulty or affliction affect your every moment? Do you live alone? Are your days or your health waning? Are you stretched to the limit by the demands of each day? Identify your greatest challenge, and then look to the Lord with the greatest of faith. Remember, "faith is the substance of things hoped for, the evidence of things not seen" (Hebrews 11:1).

Rebekah

~

Remarkable Journey

Ready, Willing, and Able!

And Rebekah said, "I will go."
GENESIS 24:58

~

Some of my most joyous days of ministry to women were those I spent with the single women in the church where my husband Jim pastored a group of precious single saints. The blessing of knowing and serving alongside the remarkable women in that class is still one of God's treasured blessings to me. Each and every one of them was one of God's special servants, a "Rebekah," if you will. Let me explain by showing you another one of God's special servants.

Ready to Serve

We meet only a handful of single women in Scripture, but in Genesis 24 God presents Rebekah, a stunning woman of faith and service, who is single. Marvel now as you meet the lovely Rebekah. Marvel at these qualities that make her one of God's special servants.

> ❧ *Rebekah's purity*—She was "a virgin; no man had known her" (Genesis 24:16).

> 🌾 *Rebekah's busyness*—Rather than looking for a husband or languishing, moping, or mourning over the lack of one, Rebekah stayed busy serving her family and others (verses 15 and 24).

> 🌾 *Rebekah's hospitality*—Her home was open to those who needed care (verse 25).

> 🌾 *Rebekah's energy*—Abundant energy is generally a sign of happiness, and Rebekah's happiness empowered her with energy enough to serve other people far beyond the minimum. Rebekah ministered to the maximum (verses 18-20)!

Before journeying on with the remarkable Rebekah, take a moment to note God's beautiful plan for His single women. God calls His special servants to a life of:

> 🌾 *Purity*—A single Christian woman is to remain "holy both in body and in spirit" (1 Corinthians 7:34).

> 🌾 *Ministry*—A single Christian woman is to live her life in a way that reflects her complete dedication to God. As one who is unmarried, she has the privilege of undistracted service to God and caring for "the things of the Lord" (1 Corinthians 7:34). Every day a woman is single is another glorious day to serve God wholeheartedly and without distraction. Her singleness is her "green light" from God to go all out in service to others.

Checkpoint on the Journey

Is singleness a reality for you today, dear woman of God? Although you may desire to be married, "let not your longing slay the appetite of your living....Accept and thank God for what is *given,* not allowing the *not-given* to spoil it."[1]

Willing to Go

Each of my daughters constantly asked me during their growing-up years, "Mom, how will I know when I've met the right man to marry? How will I know he's the right one?" And my answer was always the same, "Oh, you'll know!"

Now, let's turn that question around and ask, How does a man find a wife? This was the predicament the patriarch Abraham found himself in. But the wife he needed to find was not for himself. She was for his only son, 37-year-old Isaac. "Who?" and "How?" were the questions that plagued Abraham.

Realizing that the continuation of his family line and the fulfillment of God's promise to make his family a great nation (Genesis 12:2) were at risk, Abraham called in his oldest servant, the faithful Eliezer. After receiving a solemn oath from Eliezer, Abraham sent his 85-year-old servant on a 500-mile journey to find a wife for Isaac. This woman would have to be willing—and able!—to follow Eliezer back across those 500 miles to an unknown future in order to serve God with a man she had yet to meet. What requirements did God and Abraham set down for such a woman?

> ♪ *She must not be a Canaanite.* Abraham carefully stipulated that his servant not take a wife from the daughters of the Canaanites (Genesis 24:3). A wife from among these pagan, godless people might lead Isaac and his offspring away from the true God.

> ♪ *She must be from among Abraham's own family.* He instructed Eliezer, "You shall go to my country and to my family" (verse 4).

> ♪ *She must be willing to follow Eliezer* back to the land of Abraham and Isaac. "Willing to follow me to this land" (verse 5), Eliezer had said. A woman who would do this would be a woman willing to forsake all—in faith—for the glorious future God had ordained.

Checkpoint on the Journey

And now, dear friend, how would you describe your own devotion to God, your willingness to seek after and follow God's will for your life? Are you steadfastly renouncing the world and its influence, turning your back on its standards? Are you actively following the God of the Bible, the God you so love? As such a woman, you have a tremendous and godly influence on your world, your husband, and your children. And you have a glorious future in store!

Godly in Character

Imagine now what kind of "Wanted" poster Abraham's faithful servant might have put up on a palm tree in downtown Nahor as he looked for a wife for Abraham's son—that is, if he hadn't already spotted the real thing in Rebekah!

Wanted: The Ideal Wife

Must be physically strong and healthy,
energetic and able to work hard.
Must be friendly and industrious,
kind and compassionate,
generous and love to serve—
and devoted to God.

Abraham's faithful servant Eliezer would be listing the qualities he was searching for in his quest for a wife for Isaac, his master's only son. Sent by Abraham on a grueling 500-mile journey to find such a wife, Eliezer stopped (perhaps in the shade of a palm tree) to finalize his checklist. He was tired and thirsty after his extensive trip, and so were his ten camels. So Eliezer and his camel caravan stood at the well outside the city of Nahor.

At this point, Eliezer did one more thing with his "want" list: He lifted it up before Abraham's omniscient, omnipotent God in prayer. He knew that only God could lead him, a stranger in a strange land, to such a woman. So he asked God to "please give me success this day" (verse 12).

Considering the items on—and not on—Eliezer's list, how could God not answer his request! For instance,

> ♪ Eliezer did not mention outward appearance or material wealth.

> ♪ He asked only for godly character qualities.

> ♪ He asked for physical attributes that would enable a woman to endure an inevitably difficult life.

Checkpoint on the Journey

What does your "want" list look like? Who do you want to be? Single or married, are you focusing on godly character rather than on beauty or affluence? Would you rather be kind and loving (Galatians 5:22), or assertive and successful? Pray about your desires, and then adjust your standards to match the qualities God desires in His women. He says, "Do not let your adornment be merely outward—arranging the hair, wearing gold, or putting on fine apparel—rather let it be the hidden person of the heart, with the incorruptible beauty of a gentle and quiet spirit, which is very precious in the sight of God" (1 Peter 3:3-4).

Able to Work

Rightly or wrongly, we tend to evaluate a person's character based upon our first meeting with him or her. And that first impression can be very important. It was no different when Abraham's servant first saw Rebekah. Tired from a long journey and on a mission to find a bride for Isaac, the only heir to Abraham's wealth and God's promise, Eliezer waited by the town well in Nahor for the young women to come draw water (Genesis 24:11). I should say Eliezer waited *and prayed*, asking God to bring a woman who would offer him a drink of water (verse 14). And before he had finished speaking to the Lord, "Behold, Rebekah...came out with her pitcher on her shoulder" (verse 15).

What first impression of this young woman did Abraham's servant have? And what does her initial appearance suggest about the lovely Rebekah?

Eliezer saw right away that Rebekah was a working woman: "Rebekah came out with her pitcher." At the appointed time, probably twice a day, she took her heavy clay pitcher to the town's water source to draw some precious water and carry it back to her home within the walled city. Rebekah helped care for her family by regularly drawing the water they needed.

Dear one, take a long look at Rebekah. Gaze upon her remarkable qualities of diligence and faithfulness. Watch carefully her tireless industry and humble willingness to engage in menial work. Marvel at her fine ability to do very demanding work. Wonder at her servant heart that placed the needs of her family above any concern about what others would think of her.

Checkpoint on the Journey

Do you think hard work is degrading? Do you think hard work is to be done by other people, not you? Do you dread rolling up your sleeves and working hard on some necessary task? Here, in God's Word, God praises the enchanting Rebekah. So if you are ever tempted to disdain your work, allow God's thoughts about yet another of His remarkable women—the Proverbs 31 woman—to correct your thinking: She "willingly works with her hands....She girds herself with strength, and strengthens her arms....Strength and honor are her clothing" (Proverbs 31:13,17,25). God values women who work hard to serve Him and the people He puts in their lives.

Willing to Go the "Extra Mile"

"Whoever compels you to go one mile, go with him two. Give to him who asks you" (Matthew 5:41-42). Thousands of years before Jesus Christ, God's Son, uttered these words, Rebekah was putting the "extra mile" principle into practice.

To review our progress, an old man and his ten thirsty camels are lingering around a well in a city of Mesopotamia. We've already learned that the man had traveled hundreds of miles to the town of Abraham's family to find a wife for Abraham's only son. "O LORD God...please give me success this day" (Genesis 24:12), the tired servant had prayed. And behold(!), before he affixed an "amen" to his request, the beautiful Rebekah came to the well with her empty pitcher to draw water for her family.

A faithful servant, Eliezer hurried to meet her and said, "Please let me drink a little water from your pitcher" (verse 17). How did Rebekah respond? Ever gracious, helpful, and compassionate, she bade him, "Drink, my lord," and then she volunteered the second mile of service: "I will draw water for your camels also, until they have finished drinking" (verses 18-19).

How many draws of water from the well do you think Rebekah had to make to satisfy ten (yes, ten!) thirsty camels? A camel can drink as much as 25 gallons after a long journey. And yet the generous and energetic Rebekah—ever ready, willing, and able—"hastened" and "ran" back and forth from the well to the trough many times in order to satiate the weary animals (verse 20). Rebekah went many "extra miles" on that extraordinary day!

No price can be put on the sterling qualities Rebekah exhibited in her attitudes and actions that day by the well. Her servant spirit shone like the sun, revealing her sincere and good heart. She was respectful, aware of those in need, willing to help, and generous. Giving drink to the tired old man only met a fraction of his needs. So Rebekah quickly acted to water his animals, too.

Checkpoint on the Journey

Just for today, won't you follow in beautiful Rebekah's remarkable footsteps and be on the lookout for some needy person...and then do more than is needed?

～ *Rebekah's Message for Your Life Today* ～

Rebekah's sparkling ways and effervescent heart teach us much, don't they? Before we head into the loudest of her messages sent through this chapter and the busy scene at the town well, here's something else you need to know. Rather than leave the exhausted Eliezer, Rachel further cared for him by inviting him to her parents' home (verse 25). There Abraham's servant refused to eat until he had stated his business—he believed God had led him to Rebekah and that she was the one to be Isaac's wife.

What happened next, dear one, was our remarkable Rebekah taking her most remarkable step of faith, teaching us her most remarkable lesson. Despite her family's plea that she remain "just a few days" longer (Genesis 24:55), Rebekah said flat out, "I will go" (verse 58)!

Talk is one thing. Action is another—and action has always been a measure of true faith. Rebekah added her name to God's roll call of the truly faithful when she stepped out, trusting in Him. Rebekah's faith in God evidenced itself as she said, "I will go." Her words revealed much about her faith in God's leading. "I will go...with a stranger...to live in an unknown land...to be the wife of an unknown man. I will go... even though I will probably never see my family again...even though I have no time to prepare...even though the nomadic life of Abraham's family will be strenuous. I will go!"

And the end of this part of the story...and of this chapter? The next morning "they sent away Rebekah" (verse 59).

Checkpoint on the Journey

Take a serious inventory of your own life of faith. Is there any act of faith you are postponing—even for "just a few days"? Any decision you are putting off? Any step of faith you are delaying? Waiting may be easier, but the harder path of true faith is the path to greater blessing. Delayed obedience is in actuality disobedience, and delayed action delays God's blessing. Every step of faith is a giant step toward the center of God's will...and God's abundant blessings!

Tests of Faith

"And Rebekah said to Isaac, 'I am weary of my life.'"
GENESIS 27:46

~

*W*e never know what a day holds, do we? But an ordinary day can mark the beginning of an extra-ordinary journey! That's what happened to Rebekah. How could she have known that on that ordinary day back in her hometown, an ordinary trip to the town well would change the course of the history of the world? Rebekah had simply gone—as she did every day of her life—to draw water for the household. Yet, on that God-appointed day, a stranger was waiting there...and, well, the rest is history!

As our Rebekah began her remarkable journey into God's will, her beloved family stood on the road and called out their blessings for her life to come:

> *Our sister, may you become*
> *the mother of thousands of ten thousands.*
> Genesis 24:60

And it happened just as they said. Rebekah became the mother of millions! Their prayers for Rebekah echoed God's promise that Abraham's many descendants would be victors over all (Genesis 13:14-15; 15:5).

But wait, we're getting ahead of the story. Before she became a mother, Rebekah had to become a wife!

How does a woman become a wife? There were many steps for our Rebekah, steps that involved prayer along with parental permission and blessing (Genesis 24:60). With these important preliminaries taken care of, Rebekah set off on her journey of faith. From that point on it went like this for Rebekah…as she encountered one test of her faith after another.

Test #1—Leaving All

Every healthy marriage involves "leaving and cleaving," and it was no different for Rebekah's. After a bittersweet farewell to her family and a long journey through the desert, Rebekah caught the first glimpse of Isaac, her husband-to-be. He was in the fields that evening as her caravan moved slowly toward the end of the strenuous 500-mile trek from her home to his. Isaac, who was walking and meditating, praying and waiting, spotted the camels coming. "Could it be?" he wondered. Was it possible the old servant had found a bride for him?

God be praised! The answer to both heart cries was yes! So Isaac "took Rebekah and she became his wife, and he loved her" (Genesis 24:67). One of God's remarkable women of faith all those ages ago, Rebekah took the next step in God's divine design for her life. On that day, surely Rebekah hoped to be the kind of wife God wanted her to be!

Checkpoint on the Journey

If you, too, are married, take to heart these guidelines from God:

> ⚘ "*Leave*" your family and "cleave" to your husband. When you marry, you are freed forever from the authority of your parents and joyfully bound to your husband. He—not your father or mother, brothers or

sisters—is to be the most important person in your life (Genesis 2:24).

❧ *Help* your husband. God has ordained your role as one of helping, of using your energy to assist your husband with his responsibilities, his tasks, his goals (Genesis 2:18).

❧ *Follow* your husband. Only one person at a time can successfully lead any organization or institution and, in your home, God has given that difficult role of leadership to your husband. Your role is to follow (Genesis 3:16; Ephesians 5:22).

❧ *Respect* your husband. How lovely it is to be in the presence of a wife who respects her husband! She shows her respect. She speaks it. She treats her husband as she would treat Christ Himself. This is God's lovely, high calling for you too, dear wife (Ephesians 5:33).

Test #2—Barrenness

God's ways are not our ways (Isaiah 55:8-9), and God's timing is not always our timing (Ecclesiastes 3:1). Isaac's beautiful bride Rebekah had to learn these two lessons about God's plans. You see, their marriage made in heaven had one flaw. Twenty years passed and there was no baby. No baby to love. No baby to continue the family line. No baby to stand as a flesh-and-blood testimony of God's faithfulness to His promise (Genesis 12:2). As God reports it, "she was barren" (Genesis 25:21)...and that was a test for Rebekah.

Consider how such heartache is often handled today. Doctors are consulted. Parents are informed. Best friends are updated daily. Husbands can become the target of much anger, blaming, belittling, and criticism. Emotions swing from shock to sorrow, from fear to panic. Arguments and complaints, mixed with tears of discouragement and depression, ring through homes where the happy blessing of children has been withheld.

What word of advice would God's couple, Rebekah and Isaac, have for us today when our dreams are thwarted? In a word, *pray*. "Now Isaac *pleaded* with the LORD for his wife, because she was barren; and the LORD granted his plea, and Rebekah his wife conceived" (verse 21). We don't know how many prayers for how many years were lifted to God on Rebekah's behalf, but we do know that prayer was the means by which Rebekah entered into God's plan and His timing. Indeed, God's ways and His will come in His own perfect time.

> Like coral strands beneath the sea,
> So strongly built and chaste,
> The plans of God, unfolding, show
> No signs of human haste.[1]

Checkpoint on the Journey

For what are you waiting, dear one? Leave the desires of your heart with God through prayer and live each day in full contentment and confidence that your life—just as it is—is a part of God's perfect plan and His perfect timing. With prayer you can enjoy God's peace that passes all understanding (Philippians 4:7)...for one more day...for as many days as God's plan and God's timing takes!

Test #3—A Problem Pregnancy

Each year of its life, a tree grows new wood. The new wood nourishes the roots, fruit, and flowers, which are evidence that growth has occurred. Like a tree, Rebekah was also growing as she learned new lessons for life. One of those lessons was that prayer is the best way to handle the events and difficulties of life. The two major blessings in her life had indeed happened when people prayed:

- ❧ The blessing of marriage—Abraham's servant had prayed for a bride for Isaac...and God had led him to Rebekah (Genesis 24). Prayer was a key factor in Rebekah becoming Isaac's wife.

- ❧ The blessing of children—When Rebekah was still barren after 20 years of marriage, Isaac prayed to God...and she conceived. Prayer was a primary reason she was pregnant.

But now something was wrong. Rebekah was pregnant, and it was a problem pregnancy. Feeling an uneasy commotion in her body, she wondered, "If all is well, why am I like this?" (Genesis 25:22).

As the pregnancy and her worries continued, the blossoming fruit of spiritual growth burst forth: Rebekah "went to inquire of the LORD" (verse 22). Her understanding of God's power encouraged her to depend on Him more fully. And she was not disappointed. The Lord spoke to her (verse 23).

Checkpoint on the Journey

You can be confident that God listens to your prayers when you call on Him (Psalm 4:3). Like Rebekah, you too can grow to depend more fully on God's power and His love by praying in your difficulties. Such asking in prayer helps you look at your problem in light of God's power, instead of looking at God in the shadow of your problems. Asking in prayer reaps other fruit, too:

- ❧ Prayer deepens your insight into what you really need.

- ❧ Prayer broadens your appreciation for God's answers.

- ❧ Prayer allows you to mature so you can use His gifts more wisely.[2]

Rebekah's problem was a problem pregnancy. What is yours? Whatever your pain or problem, trial or temptation, suffering or sorrow, follow in Rebekah's footsteps of faith and inquire of the Lord. Ask in prayer. As the familiar hymn advises, "Take it to the Lord in prayer."

Test #4—Family Problems

And exactly what was the outcome of Rebekah's prayers?

First, only God could know that Rebekah was carrying twins. God forms the inward parts of each child in the womb of its mother, and its frame is not hidden from Him. Rebekah's twins were the first recorded in Scripture, and only God could give her that information (see Psalm 139:13-16).

Second, only God could know the futures of her twin sons. God's answer to Rebekah's question, "Why am I this way?" (Genesis 25:22) contained a prophecy regarding her twins: "Two nations are in your womb, two peoples shall be separated from your body; one people shall be stronger than the other, and the older shall serve the younger" (verse 23). Her twins would reverse the traditional roles—the older would serve the younger—and the two would struggle as each became a great nation.

That doesn't sound so bad, does it? So, what's the big problem? Beloved, an entire *book* could be written on the pain Rebekah's problem children brought to her heart, her marriage, and the world! We won't go into depth about the lifelong conflict between Jacob and Esau, Rebekah's twin sons. And time and space do not permit an in-depth discussion of Rebekah's role in promoting the conflict between the two brothers. But here's a list of the sorrows that soon became the constant atmosphere in Rebekah's home-sweet-home.

partiality	favoritism
profanity	jealousy
strife	lying

deception	confusion
trouble	alienation
indulgence	injustice
misery	sin
evil	grief
separation	heartache

Rebekah's beautiful marriage and her hopes of a beautiful family life turned sour. Her own words declare her anguish—"I am weary of my life" (Genesis 27:46).

Checkpoint on the Journey

Rebekah exhibited her faith in God by praying to Him and inquiring of Him. When perplexed, disturbed, anxious, and distressed, she turned her anxiety into asking. Why not make it your practice to do the same—to turn your anxiety into asking? Why not take your problems and struggles and routinely...

go into the sanctuary of God (Psalm 73:17),
spread out your case before the Lord (2 Kings 19:14),
and ask counsel at the Almighty's throne
(Hebrews 4:16)?

Test #5—Too Beautiful

Like any year of your life, each year of Rebekah's life brought many tests of her faith. So far, she had successfully weathered a series of significant faith tests.

> ♣ *Separation*—Rebekah had left family and homeland to marry the only son of Sarah and Abraham, the sole heir to God's promise to make Abraham's descendants into a great nation (Genesis 12:2).

≈ *Marriage*—In time, Rebekah had made the necessary adjustments to married life and to her marriage partner.

≈ *Childlessness*—Two decades passed as Rebekah waited for a child, waited for the promise, waited on God—and learned the lessons of faith that only waiting can teach (Genesis 25:21).

≈ *Motherhood*—Finally, not one, but two babies had been born! Being the mother of the world's first-recorded set of twins had stretched Rebekah's faith to greater lengths...and would continue to until she died.

The only thing about Rebekah that wasn't weathering with time was her exquisite appearance. But her enduring beauty presented yet another test of faith for Rebekah.

The setting for the test was a famine in the land. God specifically instructed Rebekah's husband to stay where he was during the famine. So Isaac—by *faith*—had stayed, but—in *fear*—he had lied about Rebekah. He said to the king of the Philistines, "'She is my sister'; for he was afraid to say, 'She is my wife,' because he thought, 'lest the men of the place kill me for Rebekah, because she is beautiful to behold'" (Genesis 26:7). (Does any of this sound familiar?!)

Checkpoint on the Journey

What would you have done? How do you normally face fear (not to mention betrayal!)? Do you panic? Flee? Crumble? Through the ages, God's women have chosen to trust God (1 Peter 3:6). The next time you are frozen with fear, remember—faith fights fear. Fight your fears with God's formula for your faith—T-R-U-S-T:

T*rust in God*—not your husband (1 Peter 3:1-2).

R*efuse to succumb to fear* (1 Peter 3:6).

Understand that God always protects you (Psalm 23:4).

Strengthen your spirit with God's promises (2 Peter 1:4).

Thank God for His promised protection (Isaiah 41:10).

∼ *Rebekah's Message for Your Life Today* ∼

Everyone struggles...and so did Rebekah. And every struggle is a test of our faith. We struggle in marriage, with finances, with health problems, with family members, in our career, in our job, with friends, and with temptation. Rebekah's life certainly didn't turn out as she wished! She failed in many ways as a wife and mother, but through her remarkable life's journey with its hills and valleys, you and I learn many life-messages.

1. Decisions must be guided by God's Word.

2. Problems must be prayed over.

3. Marriages must be worked at.

4. Children must be raised without favoritism.

5. God must be trusted at all times.

Jochebed

~

Remarkable Mother

The Heart of a Mother

"She hid him three months."
EXODUS 2:2
~

*M*any wonder what true faith looks like in real, everyday life. As you meet Jochebed, our next remarkable woman in the Bible, you find a picture of faith in action. Related to the patriarchs of the faith, Abraham, Isaac, and Jacob, this mother was forced to put faith into action.

The Faith of a Mother

As the mother of a newborn boy, Jochebed was faced with a frightening dilemma. The pharaoh had ordered that every son born of the Jews should be cast into the Nile River (Exodus 1:22), but could she let her son die?

Motivated by her trust in God and her love for her child, Jochebed took a step of remarkable faith and hid her little Moses instead (Exodus 2:2).

As we head into this faith-stimulating look at the great mother-of-faith Jochebed, think a minute about your faith. What would people point to in your life as evidence of a strong faith? What acts or choices of faith (James 2:22) might they have noticed? Jochebed shows you how to hold up your frightening, seemingly impossible situations to your Father in heaven. Worry ends when faith begins...and that faith ends when worry begins. So make a decision to face your trials with courage fueled by faith. Make a decision to refuse to fear and to instead place your trust in God. Declare with David, "Whenever I am afraid, I will trust in You" (Psalm 56:3). Join with Jochebed in a life of real, everyday faith.

The Courage of a Mother

"Cast your bread upon the waters, for you will find it after many days" (Ecclesiastes 11:1). This principle for living a life of faith alludes to the agricultural practice of throwing seed upon water or soggy ground and then waiting for it to produce a harvest. You, too, at times must step out with the courage of faith before you can receive God's blessing.

Like a farmer, Jochebed was forced to take a chance with her seed, but her "seed" was her tiny baby Moses. The pharaoh of Egypt had ordered every male baby born to the Jews to be drowned in the Nile River (Exodus 1:22). Jochebed, however, put her faith in God to work at once and hid her dear little one for three months. (That was the easy part!)

Soon, however, she had to take another risk of faith. Realizing she could no longer hide a vigorous infant, and trusting God, Jochebed "took an ark of bulrushes...put the child in it, and laid it in the reeds by the river's bank" (Exodus 2:3). She was casting her bread—her beloved son—upon the waters!

But Jochebed's courage paid off. In His great providence, God brought the pharaoh's own daughter to the riverbank. She found the ark and had compassion for the infant inside. Needing a nursemaid for the baby, the princess next found Jochebed—further evidence of God's providence. In the end, due to her courage (and God's goodness!), Jochebed was allowed to keep and nurse the precious babe she had placed into the hands of God when she had placed him in the river. Truly—and literally—Jochebed had cast her seed upon the waters...and it came back to her.

What challenge in your life requires a courageous risk of faith from you? Are you sending your own child off to school or college, off to married life, off to a job in another city or state, off to serve God on the mission field or in the military? Do you feel like you are losing him or her? Have the faith of Jochebed—the courage that casts your bread upon the water. Trust God that you will eventually reap benefits and blessings because of your risk of faith.

The Time of a Mother

If you are a mother, grandmother, or aunt, God's high calling for you is to devote yourself and your time to those children during the first few years of their lives. God has given you the important role of teaching His little ones, of informing them about Him, of nurturing them up for Him, of giving Him a godly man or woman to use for His great purposes. And Jochebed shows us how!

Her name—Jochebed is the first person in Scripture to have a name compounded with *Jah*, or *Jehovah*. *Jochebed* means "glory of Jehovah," "Jehovah is her glory," or "Jehovah is our glory."[1] It was to such a remarkable woman of God—a woman whose glory is Jehovah—that the pagan daughter of the pharaoh said, "Take this child away and nurse him for me" (Exodus 2:9).

Her son—Little did the pharaoh's daughter know that the infant she had just taken out of the basket she had found floating in the Nile River was Jochebed's own baby!

Her assignment—The opportunity to nurse little Moses gave Jochebed approximately three years to teach her son the great truths about Jehovah, "her glory." Jochebed had just a little time, just a few years, to give God a man who would lead His people. Then she would have to deliver him to the pharaoh's daughter to be raised in a godless home.

Just a few years! Do you know that 50 percent of a child's character and personality development takes place by age three and 75 percent by age five? The first years of a child's life are critical years for input and training. Jochebed was one of God's faithful mothers who devoted her time those first critical years to train her son in the ways of the Lord. Indeed, the only time that she had with her little boy was those few years. If you're a mom, please take seriously your calling as a mother. Just a few years of time devoted to God's little ones makes a world of difference!

The Training of a Mother

God has given Christian mothers the sacred assignment of training up their children for Him. Proverbs 22:6 spells it out this way: "Train up a child in the way he should go."

The Bible tells us Jochebed "took the child and nursed him" (Exodus 2:9). This godly mother trained up her little Moses for his first three years, and we can be sure her heart was heavy the day she gave him over to the pharaoh's daughter for the rest of his life. But we clearly see that Jochebed's faithful training lasted because, later, Moses' life exemplified the second half of Proverbs 22:6—"And when he is old he will not depart from it." At 40 years of age, Moses chose to identify with God's people rather than remain in the pharaoh's palace (Hebrews 11:24-26), and that was the first step toward the important role God had for him.

God gives mothers two basic guidelines for training up their children in Deuteronomy 6:5-7:

> *Love God*—"You shall love the LORD your God with all your heart, with all your soul, and with all your

strength." Dear heart, devote yourself to your heavenly Father. Love Him more than anyone or anything else!

Teach God's Word—"You shall teach [My words] diligently to your children, and shall talk of them when you sit in your house, when you walk by the way, when you lie down, and when you rise up." Faithfully communicate the truths of Scripture to your children.

Is pleasing your heavenly Father the overarching concern of your life? With a deep love for God as the foundation of your life and His Word hidden in your heart, you definitely have something to impart to your children. So in the day-in, day-out routines of home life you must consciously—and constantly—talk to your children about God! By doing so, you train a child for God.

Every single day counts in training up a child for God. Jochebed had only about 1000 days with her little Moses. How many do you have left? Make each one of them count!

The Work of a Mother

Turn on the news. Read any newspaper. Evil is a fact of life in this fallen world. Jochebed, too, lived in an evil world that was growing darker every day. When her third baby was born, the pharaoh in Egypt put forth his evil hand of oppression to harm God's people (Exodus 1:11), ordering that every boy born to the Jews be murdered (Exodus 1:16,22). What could Jochebed—a godly woman and devoted mother—do against such evil? Her solution was to put to work all that God had worked in her:

> ♪ *Courage*—As we've already noted, Jochebed decided to keep her baby and put her faith to work rather than kill him, thereby preserving him to bless the world.

 ♪ *Creativity*—Jochebed went to work and made a basket from bulrushes, covered it with tar and mud, and then put her baby in it to keep him alive as he floated upon the Nile River (Exodus 2:3).

 ♪ *Care*—During the brief time she had him, Jochebed did the work of lovingly nursing and diligently training her little son in the ways of the Lord.

 ♪ *Confidence*—Jochebed then did her toughest "work-of-faith" and placed her son in the pharaoh's household while placing her confidence in God, trusting that He would care for her boy. "She brought [Moses] to Pharaoh's daughter" (verse 10).

In the end, God used Jochebed's courage, creativity, care, and confidence to position her son Moses inside the house of the pharaoh. God would one day use Moses to fight against evil and save His people from Egyptian oppression.

If you are a mother, "do not fret because of evildoers" (Psalm 37:1). Instead, do the work of a mother and devote yourself to raising godly children. The prince of darkness is helpless against the power of the truth you plant in your child's heart and mind. Be courageous, be creative, care for your children, and place your complete confidence in God.

The Legacy of a Mother

The Bible doesn't say much about the godly mother Jochebed, but the lives of her three children speak volumes. And what a legacy! Exactly who were her celebrated children?

 ♪ *Aaron,* her firstborn, became Israel's first high priest, marking the beginning of the Aaronic priesthood (Exodus 30:30).

 ♪ Her daughter, *Miriam,* was a gifted poetess and musician who led the Israelite women in a victory song after

God delivered them from the pharaoh's army (Exodus 15:20) and who, with her brothers, was intimately involved in God's deliverance of Israel from Egyptian oppression. (You'll get to know Miriam better in our next chapter.)

 ᔕ *Moses,* the small baby that Jochebed gave to the pharaoh's daughter in order to save his life (Exodus 2:10), was used by God to lead His people out of Egypt and to communicate to them His fundamental commands for life (Exodus 4:11-12; 24:3).

From whom did these three inherit their legacy, their flame of faith? From their mother, Jochebed! She had taken seriously her relationship with God and her calling as a mother. She had lived her life as unto the Lord, and her sons and daughter lighted their torches of faith at her flame.

You and I are called to light the fires of faith in our homes. To do so, we ourselves must burn energetically with a hot love for the Lord, with the bright joy of our salvation, with a shining commitment to our family. Being such a fire of faith is costly because light comes at the cost of that which produces it. But as we give our lives to fuel the flame of faith in those we love most, as we burn brilliantly and intensely, our children will have the opportunity to inherit the flame of our love for God and our faith in Him. The legacy of a love for God will be passed on.

The Heart of a Mother

As we look into the heart of this remarkable mother, we see that truly, she is one of the great and godly mothers found in the Bible. Her vocation and passion can be summarized in a single word—*mother.* Perhaps these modern-day "commandments" for mothers will help as you, like Jochebed, nurture your own fierce, godly mother-heart.

Commandment #1: Begin early—"Let every Christian parent understand when the child is three years old that they have done more than half they ever will for his character."[2]

Commandment #2: Embrace motherhood as an occupation—"The most important occupation on the earth for a woman is to be a real mother to her children. It does not have much glory in it; there is a lot of grit and grime. But there is no greater place of ministry, position, or power than that of a mother."[3]

Commandment #3: Live a life of integrity—"Only as genuine Christian holiness and Christlike love are expressed in the life of a parent, can the child have the opportunity to inherit the flame and not the ashes."[4]

Commandment #4: Partner with God—"Parenthood is a partnership with God. You are not molding iron nor chiseling marble; you are working with the Creator of the universe in shaping human character and determining destiny."[5]

God's calling to teach and train those little ones He gives to us makes it vital that we nurture in our heart a fierce passion for God's Word, for His wisdom, and for our dear children.

∾ Jochebed's Message for Your Life Today ∾

We've already become acquainted with Hebrews, chapter 11, "God's Hall of Fame" or "God's Hall of Faith." We've admired dear Sarah's portrait hanging there as a woman of remarkable faith. But now, as we continue walking through God's gallery of faith's heroes, we must pause before His glowing portrait of Jochebed. Hers is labeled *the portrait of a remarkable mother*. As we look at Jochebed's picture, we behold a quiet strength in her—the strength that comes with faith in our unchanging God:

ॐ *Faith of her fathers*—Both her father, Levi, and her brother, Kohath, were priests—a fact that suggests much about Jochebed's heritage and upbringing. Hers was a family set apart to serve the Lord!

ॐ *Faith as a wife*—When Jochebed became the wife of Amram, also a priest, her faith joined with his, and another family of faith was born.

ॐ *Faith as a mother*—Jochebed passed her godly heritage on to her three children, Aaron, Moses, and Miriam. Aaron and Moses were priests, and Miriam served alongside them (Micah 6:4). But long before the three of them began serving the Lord, we see their mother Jochebed's greatest act of faith in defying the pharaoh's command.

We've grown much already by heeding the messages from God's remarkable women of the Bible shot straight from God's heart...to their hearts...to our hearts. But what can we do to further grow in our love for God and our faith in Him? To grow a heart of great women such as Jochebed, we can...

— Look for ways to spend more time in God's Word. Empowered by His Holy Spirit, the truth of Scripture at work in your heart will help you to be strong and stand fast in the faith (1 Corinthians 16:13), thus living out a strong and godly example of steadfast faith.

— Look for ways to live out your faith. Even seemingly small choices can require a measure of faith and courage, and those situations can help perfect our faith. As we focus on God's all-sufficient power and grace, problems dim and obstacles diminish as He demonstrates His faithfulness and our faith in Him grows.

Miriam

~

Remarkable Leader

A Devoted Sister

"And his sister stood afar off,
to know what would be done to him."
EXODUS 2:4

～

C hristian mothers wonder daily, How can I nurture family values in my home? How can I promote concern for one another among my children? How can I raise my children to love each other? Before we look at some of God's answers to these vital questions, note how one devoted sister models such family values for us.

Tender Loving Care

Her name is Miriam. And Miriam was a 12-year-old girl who undoubtedly adored her new baby brother. For three months she helped her mother, Jochebed, hide little Moses and care for him as their family defied the pharaoh's edict to kill every newborn Hebrew boy (Exodus 1:22). Then her mother placed the infant into a floating basket that she set among the reeds of the Nile River. Miriam "stood afar off, to know what would be done to him." Then, when the opportunity arose—when the pharaoh's daughter discovered the baby—Miriam approached her and offered to find a nurse for the infant, thereby arranging for her baby brother to be cared for at home again (Exodus 2:2-9).

Now, where do you think young Miriam developed such family loyalty? Probably from her wonderful mother. And, as the mother in your home—or as a devoted grandmother or aunt—you, too, can help instill such values in your family. Daily efforts to do the following will help:

- Teach siblings to love one another (John 15:12,17). Encourage brothers and sisters to pray for one another and to do secret acts of kindness for one another.

- Openly express kindness and concern for others (Proverbs 12:25). Children repeat what they hear and mimic what they see. So be a living model of Jesus Christ, acting with His kindness and compassion.

- Express love openly. Be affectionate and verbal. Say "I love you" every time you say goodbye or talk on the phone to your children.

- Cultivate strong family ties. Develop a "three musketeers mentality" of "one for all and all for one." See that each family member supports and encourages the others.

- Pray for God's love to be made manifest by your children (Galatians 5:22).

And remember, too, that the effective, fervent prayer of a righteous mother avails much (James 5:16)!

A Mirror of Her Mother's Merits

Traditionally, Jewish girls remained under the care and guidance of their mothers until marriage. So for a dozen years already, Jochebed had trained her daughter Miriam in the vital

qualities of diligence, faithfulness, responsibility, and wisdom—
and young Miriam clearly exhibited these virtues. She became
a mirror of her mother's remarkable merits. Here's how her
opportunity to shine unfolded.

As we've learned, the pharaoh had commanded that every
boy born to the Hebrews be drowned in the Nile River, and
Moses' parents had defied that edict. Instead, they had hidden
Moses until he could no longer be kept secret. Then came the
sad day when they placed Moses in a basket on the river—and
into the hands of God.

Perhaps Moses' mother couldn't bear to watch what might
happen to her dear baby. Or perhaps her presence at the riverbank would be too obvious. Or perhaps Jochebed asked her
daughter Miriam to stand nearby and watch over the basket. Or
perhaps the spunky and devoted sister felt compelled to stay
and look out for her baby brother. However it happened, the
young girl "stood afar off, to know what would be done to
him" (Exodus 2:4).

As Miriam peered through the reeds, the daughter of the
pharaoh came to bathe. Curious about the floating basket, the
princess opened it up, and Moses began to cry. The baby
needed milk.

At that moment Miriam stepped forward and cleverly asked,
"Shall I go and call a nurse for you from the Hebrew women,
that she may nurse the child for you?" (verse 7). Given permission by the princess, Miriam brought Jochebed—her mother
and Moses' mother—to feed him. Because of Miriam's quick
thinking, a triple blessing was reaped by her family:

- Moses' life was saved.

- Jochebed received her baby back.

- Jochebed even received wages from the pharaoh's
  daughter for nursing Moses (verse 9)!

Teaching your children love, mercy, caring, and compassion along with diligence, faithfulness, responsibility, and wisdom—the kinds of traits we see in Miriam—begins with you, dear mom. Your children will mirror your merits. What are they seeing in you and learning from your actions? Whatever you sow, that shall you also reap (Galatians 6:7)!

Devotion to God and to Ministry

"Miriam, what advice do you have for a single woman?" Imagine an interviewer today asking this question of Miriam, one of God's super-singles of yesterday. What wisdom do you think Miriam would offer after her 90-plus years of singleness?

Perhaps Miriam would say simply, "Devote yourself to God and to ministry." The Bible provides no evidence that Miriam ever married. In all of Scripture, no husband or children are mentioned. But apparently, rather than pining away or giving in to feelings of inferiority, hopelessness, or loneliness, Miriam viewed her singleness as an opportunity to give herself fully to God. As a result, she blossomed into one of the Bible's strongest female leaders (Micah 6:4). Throughout the deliverance of God's people from Egyptian bondage and their journey into the Promised Land, Miriam, the sister of Moses and Aaron (Exodus 15:20), accompanied and assisted her brothers in their leadership of the Israelites.

If you are unmarried as you read these words today, may you, dear lover of God, join the ranks of Miriam. Oh, you may have your job, your career (which, remember, is also an important opportunity for ministry), but the rest of your time is labeled by time-management experts as *discretionary time*. And you are in complete control of how you use your discretionary time—that time which is yours to manage at will because it is *your time*.

So, single or married, take some time to pray about these questions:

❧ How effectively am I using my "free" time—my evenings, my weekends, my children's naptime—for God's kingdom?

❧ What doors of ministry are open to me now?

Just think of the myriad ministries you could have during your free time! You could disciple or mentor another woman in the faith. You could write or e-mail a lonely missionary. You could take a meal to a cancer patient. You could visit a shut-in. You could help your church prepare for Sunday worship services. Add your own ideas to this list of suggestions and then take a bold step...right into the realm of selfless ministry and devote yourself to helping others!

Devotion to Family

We saw the delightful, quick-thinking Miriam hide among the reeds along Egypt's Nile River. Holding her breath, she quietly watched the tiny floating basket that held her baby brother Moses, and waited to see what would happen to him (Exodus 2:4).

But Miriam's devotion to her brother Moses didn't end there on the riverbank. In response to God's call to live her life as a single woman, Miriam chose to devote herself to serving her two brothers, Aaron and Moses, as they served God and His people (Micah 6:4).

Now, did you think about the fictitious interview with Miriam, one of God's super-singles, and the question "What advice do you have for a single woman?" Based on how Miriam lived her life, we imagined that her first piece of advice would be, "Devote yourself to God and to ministry." Today we want to add her second pearl of wisdom—"Devote yourself to family."

Miriam, a woman who evidently had no husband or children, devoted her heart, her love, her energy, and her wit to helping her brothers in the massive undertaking of leading the

Jewish nation—over two million people!—out from under the oppression of the Egyptian pharaoh and into the freedom of the Lord. Apparently, as Aaron and Moses led the entire company, Miriam was looked upon—and acted as—the premier leader of the women.

So now for you, dear one. Are you single? If so, in what creative ways can you serve and support your own family members in their various endeavors, especially those laboring for God's kingdom? No one more than family deserves your loyalty and understanding!

Or are you a mother? If so, are you nurturing family unity among your children? Try to engage your family in joint service to God. Your family could, for instance, adopt a missionary family, serve a meal at a local mission, labor shoulder-to-shoulder during a church workday, attend a family camp, teach Sunday school, and fill a new backpack with school supplies for a child who wouldn't have one otherwise. As you encourage mutual service to God and mutual ministry to one another in your family, your children will be well on their way to joining together in service to God, just as Moses, Aaron, and Miriam did.

A Rare Honor

A prophetess is a woman who acts as a mouthpiece for God, receiving a message from Him and proclaiming it in accordance with His commands.[1] Only a handful of women in Scripture have received that honored role and title. They include "Miriam, the prophetess," Deborah, Huldah, Anna, and Philip's four daughters.[2] Miriam, the sister of Aaron and Moses, was the first woman to be given this rare honor as the Lord spoke through her to His people (Numbers 12:1-2). One of those occasions was a great day in the history of the Jewish people. Here's what happened....

Times were tense. The years before Miriam's prophesying included her people's bondage under the oppressive hand of the Egyptians (Exodus 1:11-14). When the sons of Israel cried out to God for help, God sent Moses and Aaron, Miriam's brothers, to lead His people to freedom (4:27-31). After ten encounters with Moses and numerous plagues choreographed by God Himself, Pharaoh finally allowed the Israelites to leave Egypt.

Yes, times were tense when Pharaoh increased the Jews' workload, withheld the supplies they needed, repeatedly changed his mind about their release, and finally, after the death of every firstborn Egyptian male, consented to their departure. But even then Pharaoh was so angry that he sent an army of warriors in pursuit of the Jews (Exodus 14:5-9).

This dramatic situation was the backdrop for one more mighty and supernatural act. As soon as all of the Jewish people walked through the miraculously parted Red Sea waters, God just as miraculously closed the waters over the entire Egyptian army (Exodus 14:28).

What wonder! What relief! What deliverance! Moses erupted into a song of sheer praise. Miriam offered her own God-inspired song, too. Hear the joyous words of Miriam the prophetess as she, with tambourine in hand and followed by all the women who were dancing and playing their own tambourines, exulted in Exodus 15:21:

> Sing to the LORD, for He has triumphed gloriously!
> The horse and its rider He has thrown into the sea!

Lessons in Leadership

Do you have aspirations for leadership? If leading other women is one of the desires of your heart, or if leadership is something you wish to pray about, consider a few principles of spiritual leadership and ask God to help grow them in your life.

> ❧ *A leader is a follower*—The adage is true that to be a leader you must first be a follower. Leadership is a

discipline, and it is in the process of being a faithful follower that you gain the discipline necessary for effective leadership.

⚘ *A leader is a pray-er*—Prayer brings to leadership the power and energy of the Holy Spirit. Missionary and leader Hudson Taylor was convinced that "it is possible to move [others], through God, by prayer alone."

⚘ *A leader is an initiator*—It is only the authentic leader who is willing to take risks and move out courageously as venturesomeness is applied to vision.[3]

If you are looking for a model of a leader of women, God shows you in Miriam one of His very special women of faith who lived out these principles of leadership. As the Bible explains, "All the women went out after her" (Exodus 15:20).

⚘ *Miriam was a follower*—She faithfully followed and assisted her two brothers, Aaron and Moses, as they led God's people to freedom (Micah 6:4).

⚘ *Miriam was a pray-er*—As a prophetess and a pray-er, Miriam was filled with the Holy Spirit, who inspired her words.

⚘ *Miriam was an initiator*—Moved by God's miraculous defeat of the Egyptian army in the midst of the Red Sea, Miriam "took the timbrel in her hand; and all the women went out after her with timbrels and with dances" (Exodus 15:20).

May God's Spirit at work in your life and the example of Miriam inspire you to serve as a leader for His kingdom.

∼ *Miriam's Message for Your Life Today* ∼

When I think of Miriam, the devoted sister who became a devoted leader, two stellar character qualities come shooting across the thousands of years that have passed since she modeled them for you and me—*service* and *energy*. These two qualities go hand-in-hand. Why? Because many women desire to serve others, but lack the energy, while others possess the energy, but fail in their concern for people. Miriam, however, shows us the beauty of both. When service and energy were mixed with a love for God and God's love at work in her, Miriam grew to become a remarkable leader.

Whether you are a Miriam-maker like Miriam's mother Jochebed was, or a Miriam-in-the-making on the way to a life of serving God, Miriam's remarkable life teaches us...

...to serve others,

...to serve family,

...to serve God, and

...to assist others in their love

and worship of God.

Dear one, whether God ever calls upon you to lead His women or not, remember that every life of remarkable love is built upon service to others and the energy to carry out that service. How are you doing in the Service Department? And in the Energy Department? Ask the God of all-sufficient and ever-abundant grace to assist you in *both* departments. Actively seek a heart like His. Actively seek a heart of loving concern for others. And actively seek God's energizing power to follow through on love's desires.

A Devoted Saint

"I sent before you Moses, Aaron, and Miriam."
MICAH 6:4

~

*W*hy is it so easy for us to let the memory of one negative action in a person's entire lifetime overshadow all of the good accomplished in that life? We'll get to that "one negative action" in Miriam's life a little later (and it was a BIG one!)...but for now—and throughout most of this lesson—I want us to concentrate on what a devoted saint dear Miriam was. No one could ever say that Miriam was not devoted to God, to her family, and to serving God's people!

A Singing Saint

Consider this thought-provoking idea: "Music is God's gift to man. It is the only art of heaven given to earth, and the only art of earth we take to heaven."[1]

Throughout time, God's people have expressed their praise and worship and joy to God through music and song. In fact, the Bible charges everything that has breath (and that includes you!) to "praise the Lord!" and to do so not only with your voice but also with the trumpet, lute, and harp, with the timbrel, stringed instruments, flutes, and cymbals (Psalm 150:1-6). It's natural to want to sing and shout whenever you experience an unspeakable blessing, and music allows us to express the purest praise to God and to participate in an activity of heaven.

Miriam, the sister of Moses and Aaron, brought a little bit of heaven down to earth through music so many thousands of years ago. As we've already learned, Miriam was the leader of the women in that two-million-plus assembly of God's people who escaped from bondage to the powerful pharaoh of Egypt. After they fled through the miraculously dry floor of the Red Sea—which just as miraculously closed in, on, and over the pharaoh's pursuant army (Exodus 12–14)—Miriam sang! The Bible reports that Miriam answered the men's song with her own (Exodus 15:21). Inspired by God, she sang and praised His power and faithfulness: "Sing to the LORD, for He has triumphed gloriously! The horse and its rider He has thrown into the sea!" (verse 21).

What was at the heart of Miriam's song? And how can you follow her joyous example of praising God in unashamed exaltation?

> ♪ *Praise God spontaneously*—Miriam grabbed a tambourine and spontaneously answered the male singers with a chorus of joyful praise (verse 20).

> ♪ *Praise God for who He is*—Miriam celebrated God's remarkable power and His unchallenged supremacy, justice, truth, and mercy.

> ♪ *Praise God heartily*—Miriam and the Israelite women sang and danced as they praised the Lord (verse 20). We New Testament believers are told, "Whatever you do, do it *heartily*, as to the Lord" (Colossians 3:23). Miriam is an Old Testament example of what doing something heartily as unto the Lord can look like.

So, my friend, follow in Miriam's musical footsteps and praise the Lord! Sing unto the Lord! Let all that is within *you* bless His holy name!

Songs in the Night

I love the joyous, grateful heart of Miriam as she expressed her appreciation to God in exultant song (Exodus 15:20-21). Indeed, she has been called "the first of the sweet singers of Israel," a woman who "sang for God, using her gift for the elevation of human souls into a higher life."[2]

But before we move on in the life of Miriam, God's devoted saint, I want us to look at another kind of singing referred to in the Bible as "songs in the night." Not every occasion in life is joyous. Both the psalmist and Job, two men who knew dark times of suffering and distress, speak of "songs in the night" (Psalm 77:6 and Job 35:10). Just as music is a wonderful avenue for sharing joy, it is a blessed avenue for expressing pain.

A Woman of Hymns

Two modern-day women have found that singing songs in the dark nights of their trials has helped them in their sorrow. The first is Elisabeth Elliot.

In 1956, Elisabeth Elliot's husband, Jim, was martyred by savage Auca Indians in Ecuador. Later, when an interviewer asked this woman why hymns are an important part of her life, Mrs. Elliot responded:

> I came from a home where we not only read the Bible every day, but we sang a hymn every day. I have learned as a result of that [practice]...hundreds of hymns. They are as much a part of my life as the Scriptures, and they have been a tremendous blessing to me in times of distress.

Elisabeth Elliot went on to say that, upon hearing that her husband might be dead, a verse of Scripture and the words of a hymn came to mind and ministered to her soul. Mrs. Elliot shares,

> Isaiah 43 says, "When thou passest through the waters, I will be with thee; and through the rivers, they shall not overflow thee." That idea is also taken up in the great hymn "How Firm a Foundation." As the stanza says,
>
>> When thro' the deep waters I cause thee to go, The rivers of sorrow shall not overflow. For I will be with thee thy trials to bless, And sanctify to thee thy deepest distress.[3]

Consider how biblical truth and how expressing that truth in "psalms and hymns and spiritual songs" (Ephesians 5:19) can undergird you, too, during your dark nights. In times of distress and discouragement, of heartache and heartbreak, in pain and in sorrow, remembering to sing songs in the night will bring comfort and hope.

"God's Songbird"

Have you noticed in your church, your Bible study, your circle of Christian friends, that women who love God tend to sing? Miriam sang when God gloriously delivered His people (Exodus 15:21). And we've learned about the "songs in the night" which Elisabeth Elliot sang after her husband was martyred for Christ. And now I want you to meet yet another woman who loved God and sang His praises—in the darkness.

Fanny Crosby was an American hymn writer who lived from 1820 until 1915. That's 95 years—and Fanny Crosby spent all but six weeks of those 95 years in complete blindness. When she was six weeks old, a doctor unwittingly caused Fanny's blindness, yet Fanny, through the eyes of her Christian faith, saw that doctor's apparent mistake as "no mistake of God's." She wrote, "I verily believe it was [God's] intention that I should live my days in physical darkness, so as to be better prepared to sing His praises and incite others to do so."[4] Note the path Fanny Crosby's life of singing in the darkness took:

- At age 8, Fanny Crosby began writing poetry.

- When she was 11, one of her poems was published.

- When Fanny was 24, she published her first book of poems.

- Throughout her life, Fanny wrote a large number of religious poems, cantatas, and many songs.

- At the time of her death, the total number of her hymns and poems of praise to her God exceeded 8000!

Truly, Fanny Crosby was a woman who loved God and trusted in His wisdom and His ways (Romans 11:33). Rather than succumb to bitterness or resentment, self-pity or regret, Fanny sang. She became God's songbird. Like the nightingale, she sang in the darkness...for 95 years.

Today, dear one, if you are facing what seems to be a tragedy, then lift a song of praise to God in that darkness. Worship Him while wandering in fogs of uncertainty. And bless God despite the blindness of your incomprehension. Your song of faith gives clear tribute to the goodness and greatness of God.

A Senior Saint

One of the most encouraging characteristics of the remarkable women in the Bible is that they loved God and served His people until they died. For instance, dear Sarah loved and served God and her family to the age of 127 (Genesis 23:1).

And now, as we begin saying farewell to Miriam, we witness yet another one of God's terrific senior saints. As you consider this remarkable woman and remarkable leader of women, please notice the many wonderful ways the over 80-years-old Miriam gave of her energies up to this point in her life. You'll want to make her pattern for senior sainthood a personal lifetime goal.

Miriam was still in love with the Lord—As the Israelites emerged from the parted waters of the Red Sea and witnessed God's destruction of their enemies, Miriam's heart burst into praise and song as she worshiped the Lord (Exodus 15:21). She shouted, "Sing to the LORD"!

Miriam was still leading the women—Ever the leader, when Miriam's hands reached for a timbrel and her soul sang in tribute to God, "all the women" joined her (verse 20).

Miriam was still serving with her brothers—In her later years she assisted both Moses and Aaron as these three siblings led God's two million people out of Egypt and toward God's Promised Land. Not only did the young Miriam care about her baby brother, Moses, as his little basket floated along the Nile River (Exodus 2:4), but the spunky, energetic Miriam continued to help Moses and Aaron by attending to the needs of the women as the Israelites began their journey through the wilderness.

Miriam was still singing praises to God—Her worship was public, expressive, exuberant, and heartfelt as she came before His presence with song. She never tired of praising Jehovah for His goodness and for His wonderful works to the children of men.

Whatever your age, dear sister, continue—to the end!—to be a woman who loves God, praises Him, and serves His people.

Epitaph

It's time now to face the fact of Miriam's one great failure—her "one negative action" that mars her memory. We've noted along the way Miriam's life of service to God. Four books of the Bible—Exodus, Leviticus, Numbers, and Micah—tell us something about Miriam, an amazing and remarkable woman who dearly loved God. Just look at her list of outstanding accomplishments for God:

- Miriam cared for her baby brother, Moses (Exodus 2:4).

- Miriam served God shoulder-to-shoulder with her two VIP brothers, Moses and Aaron, as they led God's people to freedom (Micah 6:4).

- Miriam prophesied for God, speaking and acting under His inspiration (Exodus 15:20).

- Miriam led the Israelite women in joyous worship after their deliverance from the Egyptian army (Exodus 15:20-21).

- Miriam served God into her nineties, earning for herself the tribute of "senior saint."

And yet...there was that one terrible incident when, in her jealousy, Miriam verbally attacked and criticized Moses and was severely punished by God with seven days of leprosy (Numbers 12). Miriam did not enter the Promised Land with God's people. The Bible reports that Miriam died there and was buried in Kadesh-barnea (Numbers 20:1). We don't know if there was a cause and effect between Miriam's sin and her not being allowed to enter the Promised Land. The Bible simply does not say. However, we do know that neither Moses nor Aaron entered the Promised Land either. Why? Because Miriam's two famous brothers, Moses and Aaron, had each participated in one unforgettable sin when they failed to honor the Lord in front of the Israelites (Numbers 20:2-12). Yet amazingly, we don't remember either Moses or Aaron in a bad light, and we shouldn't remember dear Miriam in a bad light either. We should learn from her sin (Deuteronomy 24:9), but we should also learn from her many remarkable achievements.

Don't you think words like these should have been engraved on Miriam's gravestone?

Here lies a remarkable woman
who loved God, her family,
and God's people,
and served them with
all her heart, soul,
mind, and strength.

Beginning today, make an effort to graciously note and remember all that is good in other people, rather than focusing on one unfortunate misstep or sin. As the Bible reminds us, "Whatever things are...noble...lovely...of good report...[and] praiseworthy—meditate on *these* things" (Philippians 4:8)!

～ Miriam's Message for Your Life Today ～

I can think of nothing worse than living your whole life and then, at life's end, realizing that there is nothing lasting that remains. Well, that was not the case with Miriam. Indeed, her lasting impact continues to affect us across the centuries. And her message is loud and clear! What do we learn from Miriam?

First, beyond your relationship to God, your family is your most important relationship. Careers are soon over. Friends come and go. But your loyal relationship with family will have lasting impact.

Next, whether you are married or single, ministry to and with God's people has lasting benefits. Miriam's decades of faithful service as a devoted saint gained momentum with each passing year. She teaches us that "seniorhood" equals "servanthood."

And finally, sin may have its consequence, but unfortunate missteps or even significant sins in ourselves or others should not be seen as final. God's grace is there to pick us up and put us back on the path to usefulness to our family and our church.

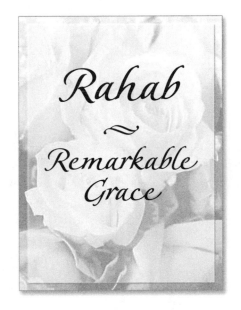

Rahab
~
Remarkable
Grace

A Cameo of Courage

Rahab "took the two men and hid them."
JOSHUA 2:4

*E*very woman loves the life story of Rahab. Why? I believe one reason is Rahab's remarkable before-and-after story. As we wonder at God's grace in Rahab's life and the remarkable person who emerged from such unlikely beginnings, keep your own before-and-after story in mind. We'll be checking it as we go.

Before and After

Rahab-the-harlot. Throughout the Bible, these three words have been used as one to refer to a remarkable woman who loved God, believed in God, and followed God...at great risk to herself. The very fact that Rahab-the-harlot appears in faith's Hall of Fame (Hebrews 11:31) signifies to us that she has a before-and-after story to tell. Consider the Bible's account of her life.

Before Rahab became a believer in the one true God, she was an idolatrous Amorite. *Ra* was the name of an Egyptian

god, and Rahab's full name meant "insolent and fierce." Besides
her less-than-positive name, the Bible reports that Rahab was
a harlot (Joshua 2:1).

But God—who, according to the pleasure of His good will,
chooses His children before the foundation of the world, that
they should be holy and without blame before Him (Ephesians
1:4-8)—touched Rahab's heart and, by His grace, transformed
her into a new creature (2 Corinthians 5:17). For Rahab, old
things passed away, and behold, all things became new!

After God's grace touched and cleansed the soul of Rahab-
the-harlot, and after her many heroic acts of faith (which we're
going to inspect one at a time), God opened the windows of
heaven and poured out His rich, abundant blessings upon her
life. What were some of the tangible blessings Rahab received
as a child of God? Quickly fast-forward in her life and marvel
at these two gracious blessings:

- Rahab married Salmon, a prince in the house of Judah.

- Rahab bore Salmon a son named Boaz...whose son
  was Obed...whose son was Jesse...whose son was
  David (Ruth 4:20-22)...through whose line Jesus was
  born (Matthew 1:1,5).

Your remarkable story—What is your personal before-and-
after story, dear one? Does it contain something as vile as
Rahab's life of prostitution? Does it include a hard spirit of
fierce insolence toward God and others? Or is it marked by an
icy, stone-cold heart toward the things of God?

Pause now and thank God for your personal before-and-
after story. The little epistle of Ephesians reminds us that in
times past (*before*), we all walked in disobedience according to
the course of this world (Ephesians 2:2). But to the praise of the
glory of His grace, God (*after*) has made us accepted in the
Beloved, accepted in His Son Jesus Christ, in whom we have

redemption through His blood—the forgiveness of sins (Ephesians 1:6-7)! Selah! Think on this!

Now, back to Rahab....

A Cameo of Courage

Most women admire a delicate and carefully crafted cameo, but few of us are aware of how that piece of jewelry comes to be so unique and beautiful. The process begins with a multi-layered stone or shell. An engraver first etches a design, usually the profile of a woman, on the piece and then sets about carving a relief in the top layer. Lower layers serve as the background for the portrait. Cutting through the tiers of colors in the stone or shell can create a striking effect, and cameos are the most breathtaking when a light color is set against a dark background.

The life of Rahab offers us one of the Bible's most dramatic cameos of courage, and what is true of a cameo was true of Rahab: Her beauty is brilliant because of the dark background against which it shines. Consider her situation.

The future was dark for Rahab and her hometown of Jericho as Joshua, the leader of God's people after Moses, sent his warrior spies into the Promised Land (Joshua 2:1). The Israelite army was planning to cross the Jordan River and take possession of their new kingdom, beginning with the godless city of Jericho.

But God, the Master Artist and Engraver, shows us in the harlot Rahab a stunning relief against the grim backdrop of godlessness, war, and impending death. We are astonished at the layer upon layer—and act upon act—of faith displayed by this unlikely woman who truly feared God.

How was Rahab's faith evidenced? What were the lovely layers of her precious faith?

When Joshua's spies entered Jericho, they "came to the house of a harlot named Rahab" (Joshua 2:1). That harlot was our Rahab, also known as Rahab-the-harlot! It was then that Rahab revealed her faith in God by hiding the two spies. As the

Bible chronicles it, "the woman took the two men and hid them" (verse 4). She then proceeded to help them escape, after eliciting from them a promise of future protection. Within the rough stone walls of a dark and godless city, the faith of one woman—a moral leper in her day—created an elegant cameo of courage for us to admire.

Your remarkable backdrop—Dear one, where do you live? And what dark events, circumstances, and trials serve as the backdrop for your daily life? How will your own precious faith shine against such layers of darkness to create an exquisite cameo of courage? God's remarkable and amazing grace is available to you, no matter how black things are!

A Statement of Faith

Almost every church and Christian organization officially declares what it believes about God and His Son. Their statements of faith include their organization's role in the world in relation to God and His Son.

Like churches and Christian associations, every woman who loves God should have a statement of faith. She should know and be able to clearly state exactly what she believes. Rahab was able to say what she believed, and one day her statement of faith saved her life. Here's how it happened.

The time had come for God's people to enter the land God had promised them. Joshua, God's appointed leader, sent two of his warriors to survey the walled city of Jericho. While these spies were staying at Rahab's house, the king of Jericho sent a message to Rahab, commanding her to hand over the men thought to be at her house. Rather than turn in the spies, though, Rahab hid them (Joshua 2:2-4).

Why did this harlot and resident of a godless town take such a risk? Hear Rahab's words to the godly spies...and her heart of faith:

❧ "I know that the LORD has given you the land" (Joshua 2:9).

❧ "We have heard how the LORD dried up the water of the Red Sea for you when you came out of Egypt" (verse 10).

❧ "The LORD your God, He is God in heaven above and on earth beneath" (verse 11).

Rahab's statements clearly reveal her knowledge of God. She obviously knew who God was and what He had done for His people. She knew of His plan to give the land to His chosen race, and she knew that God was the God of all heaven and earth. Rahab definitely had her facts about God straight!

Your statement of faith—And now for you, dear woman of faith. How would your own statement of faith read? How much do you know about God and His dealings with His people? How many of His attributes are you familiar with? How thoroughly can you spell out your knowledge of God? Take time to think...and pray...and articulate your beliefs. Search the Scriptures, too. Make it your goal to know what you believe. And then, as Rahab did, declare your faith to others!

A Handful of Choices

Rahab had no religious background, no godly heritage, no devout husband, and no pious parents. But, mark it well, Rahab's *choices* qualified her to join the ranks of Sarah, Rebekah, Jochebed, and Miriam. It's been said that *choices,* not chance, determine human destiny. We could add that, to some extent, our choices also determine our eternal destiny. Ponder the truth of these lines of poetry:

> To every man there openeth
> A Way, and ways, and a Way

> And the High Soul climbs the High Way
> And the Low Soul gropes the Low…
> But to every man there openeth
> A High Way and a Low.
> And every man decideth
> The way his soul shall go.[1]

Rahab exhibited her faith by her choices, and those choices affected her human—and her eternal—destiny. On that notable day in Jericho, when God sent His agents to Rahab's house, two ways opened up to her. The choice was hers: Would she choose the way of faith—the high way? Or would she continue on in the way of the world—the low path? Please note, as we continue to learn more about the remarkable Rahab, a handful of her brave choices—choices that revealed her remarkable faith and reaped for her a fulfilling future and eternal life.

Your remarkable choices—But before we move ahead, first consider what choices *you* are making that will affect *your* destiny. How high are your sights—and your faith—set? Are you choosing the high way? Make it your aim to choose God's way in all that you say, do, and think. That, my friend, is the *highest* way!

The Choice to Help

Most of the days of our lives move along in a predictable rhythm. We get up at a predicted time. We work our way through the day doing predictable tasks. We go to bed, finishing yet another predictable day filled with familiar people, familiar situations, and familiar activities.

And the same was true of Rahab's life. She followed along its predictable paths…until one dramatic day when she was suddenly confronted by new faces, new circumstances, and a new choice. She had heard about God and the wondrous miracles He had performed for His people—about the parting of the Red Sea and about the destruction of two Amorite kings (Joshua 2:10). But then, on one ordinary day, Rahab came face-to-face with two Israelite men...and she had a serious decision to make: Would she choose to turn the two spies over to the king's men as was demanded of her...or would she choose to help them?

Rahab chose to help the spies—Such courage and such faith! Rahab chose to risk her own life to protect her nation's enemies—the spies Joshua had sent in preparation for battle (Joshua 2:4). Hers was an act of treason, punishable by death, yet Rahab feared God more than she feared man. Such a choice revealed these fine qualities:

- *Kindness*—The two spies were in need. Rahab's king had found out about their presence. But when he asked her to deliver the men over to him, Rahab would not sacrifice their lives. Instead, she was willing to sacrifice her own.

- *Courage*—To stand up against her king and to betray her own city to death and destruction took courage. Yet Rahab acted boldly, choosing to save the two men who represented God's people. "She let them down [the wall] by a rope" (verse 15).

- *Faith*—Rahab believed. She believed what she had heard about the one true God, that He was "God in heaven above and on earth beneath" (verse 11). And she believed that her country was destined for destruction and that God and His people would prevail (verse 9).

- *Creativity*—Thinking quickly, Rahab hid Joshua's spies, sent their pursuers in another direction, and then secretly let the spies out of the city (verses 5-22).

Your choices to help—The New Testament exhorts us to "do good to all, especially to those who are of the household of faith" (Galatians 6:10). Is yours a heart that chooses to act toward God's people with kindness, courage, faith, and creativity? Do...or will...you choose to follow in the steps of Rahab in her choices to help God's people?

~ *Rahab's Message for Your Life Today* ~

How I hate to break away from Rahab's story, especially at this moment...with her life and the lives of Joshua's two courageous warriors hanging in the balance! But let's pause and listen intently to Rahab's wisdom to us, a wisdom that emerged from dark—and dire!—circumstances. If you and Rahab were having a "proverbial cup of coffee," what do you think she would say?

There's no way to miss her message of faith. Here was a woman who kept her ears—and her heart—open. She had heard all about God and His miracles on behalf of His people and against His people's enemies. She didn't write such tales off...and she didn't forget them. No, Rahab hid such astounding truths in her heart. She believed in the reports of a miracle-producing God.

How is your belief system when it comes to God and the truths reported about Him in the Bible? And how do you respond to these truths? Do you believe them? If so, then you are a true woman-of-faith, a Rahab-type woman of astounding faith.

There is one other thing I think Rahab might tell you and me. She would probably try to explain that there is faith—and then there is faith! There is faith in the truth and belief in the Word of God, the Bible, but then there is faith-in-action. You see, Rahab had both faith...and faith. And that faith was proved when Rahab heard about God and believed in Him. But faith didn't stop there. No, Rahab then went to work, took the risk, and made the choice to save the spies. Rahab lived out what the New Testament apostle James wrote, "Be doers of the word, and not hearers only, deceiving yourselves....What does it profit, my brethren, if someone says he has faith but does not have works?...Faith by itself, if it does not have works, is dead" (James 1:22; 2:14,17).

Pray, dear one! Ask God about your faith. Is it merely a "profession" of faith, or is there living proof that you are truly in "possession" of a living faith?

A Portrait of Transformation

"By faith the harlot Rahab did not perish
with those who did not believe."
HEBREWS 11:31

~

We paused after our initial look at the remarkable Rahab to contemplate a few truths about faith. As we learned, the tiny book of James explains to us that "faith by itself, if it does not have works, is dead" (James 2:17) and that "by works faith [is] made perfect" (verse 22). And, my friend, our "works" are guided by our choices.

A Chain of Choices

Have you ever thought about faith being like a chain—a series of choices linked together? Rahab, who loved God, continued to make choices that evidenced that love and her faith. We've already seen the first faith-link in her chain of choices: Rahab chose to help the spies who entered Jericho, rather than turn them over to the king. But Rahab's remarkable faith was exhibited by yet another faith choice.

Rahab chose to believe the spies—When Joshua's scouts said the Israelites would cross the Jordan River and take the land, Rahab believed them. By faith she said, "I know that the LORD has given you the land" (Joshua 2:9) and "according to your words, so be it" (verse 21). Rahab had heard of God's miraculous care for His people, was convinced of the supremacy of Jehovah, and so believed, fastening another faith link onto her growing chain of faith.

Your choice to believe—How long—and how strong—is your chain of faith? Are you an ever-growing woman of faith? Is that fact evident in the choices you make? Each sunrise, each day, each hour, and each minute brings tests to your faith, tests that call for choices, and choices that reveal belief. And, as Joshua himself later noted, you must choose whom you will serve throughout your day and with your minutes…and with your choices. Joshua passionately exhorted the Israelites to "choose for yourselves this day whom you will serve….but as for me and my house, we will serve the LORD" (Joshua 24:15).

Dear reader, what you believe and whom you serve will determine your choices and how you work out and act upon your faith—which will determine how you behave. For starters, do you believe God's Word? It's important that you do… because it makes all the difference in your choices, your faith, and your behavior! Note how believing God's Word worked positively in the lives of these two men of faith:

- ≽ Abraham, the father of our faith, believed God when He promised, "I will make you a great nation" (Genesis 12:2; 15:6).

- ≽ The apostle Paul exhibited this same faith during a storm he encountered as he sailed to Rome. He declared, "I believe God that it will be just as it was told me" (Acts 27:25).

Won't you follow in Rahab's and Abraham's and Paul's footsteps of faith and believe God's Word? The next time you have the choice of faith or doubt, choose to believe and fasten one more faith-link onto your increasing chain of faith.

Doubt sees the obstacles. *Faith* sees the way.

Doubt sees the darkest night. *Faith* sees the day.

Doubt dreads to take a step. *Faith* soars on high.

Doubt questions, "Who believes?" *Faith* answers, "I."[1]

What will your choice...and choices...be? Keep your eyes open for faith's opportunities, and keep your prayers ascending to God, "for the eyes of the LORD are on the righteous, and His ears are open to their prayers" (1 Peter 3:12). "Be strong in the Lord and in the power of His might" (Ephesians 6:10).

The Choice to Trust

Please sit back a moment and admire Rahab's remarkable faith. I know we've gone over this before, but the impact of it is mounting. Everything about Rahab's situation seemed to work against her ever becoming a woman who loved God and trusted in Him. She was a pagan, and she was a prostitute. And yet, in Hebrews 11, the chapter of the Bible considered "God's Roll Call of Faith," dear Rahab appears among the great people of faith, alongside only two other women—Sarah and Moses' mother, Jochebed. Rahab earned that place because of her choices. But now we have the opportunity to look at brave, believing Rahab-the-harlot confirm her faith by yet another choice:

Rahab chose to secure a promise—Believing in the ultimate triumph of Jehovah, Rahab asked for and received a promise from the spies that they would save her life and all her family members when they returned to annihilate the city (Joshua 2:12-14). A promise is defined as "the declaration of some benefit to be conferred."[2] Well, dear one, many of the thousands of promises in the Bible apply to you! What a blessing and a joy to partake of the many promises—those declarations of benefits to be conferred (on you!) that are based on the very nature and character of God! So make it your choice to believe these few promises:

> ✤ Jesus promised, "I will never leave you nor forsake you" (Hebrews 13:5).

> ✤ Paul promised, "My God shall supply all your need according to His riches in glory by Christ Jesus" (Philippians 4:19).

> ✤ Jesus promised, "My grace is sufficient for you" (2 Corinthians 12:9).

Your trust in God's promises—Let us again follow in the footsteps of God's beautiful woman of gracious faith, Rahab. Let us secure and appropriate God's promises for ourselves. What is God promising you today? Why not spend some time reading His Word and looking for one of His precious promises. Then, in…and by faith, make the choice to trust.

The Blessings of Belief

We're about to leave Rahab's heroic life, but not before we notice how God worked in her heart. I entitled this chapter "A Portrait of Transformation," and that's exactly what Rahab's life came to be—a portrait of remarkable faith hanging in the halls of faith and the halls of heaven. How did it happen? How did her remarkable transformation occur? Look again at her before-and-after story and at her remarkable acts of faith.

Rahab's Life Before Faith

Place of residence:	Jericho
Occupation:	Prostitute
Destiny:	Condemnation

Rahab's Acts of Faith

🎵 She helped the spies. Rather than turn Joshua's spies over to the king of Jericho, Rahab hid them, diverted the king's soldiers, and helped Joshua's men escape the city (Joshua 2).

🎵 She believed that the spies were God's people and that they would surely possess and destroy her city of Jericho (verse 9).

🎵 She secured the promise that, because of her kindness to the spies, she and her family would be spared when the soldiers returned to take the city (verses 12-14).

🎵 She acted on the promise. Immediately after the spies departed, Rahab followed their instructions and tied a scarlet cord in the window of her house—a signal that they were to save everyone in that house when destroying the city (verse 21). And the result? "Joshua spared Rahab the harlot, her father's household, and all that she had" (Joshua 6:25).

Rahab's Blessings for Faith

Rahab's remarkable story of transformation doesn't end here. Oh no! As a woman of faith (Hebrews 11:31), Rahab was greatly blessed. Hear now the end of her story (or...is it the beginning of her story?).

🎵 She and her family were spared during Jericho's destruction,

🎵 she lived in Israel the rest of her days,

🎵 she married Salmon, and

🎵 she was the mother of Boaz...who married Ruth...who bore Obed...whose son was Jesse, the father of David...through whose line came Jesus, the Messiah and Savior of the world (Matthew 1:5-6)!

Thus, by God's rich grace, Rahab's life changed. And, oh, what a remarkable transformation it was! You make the comparison...

Rahab's Life of Faith

Place of residence:	Israel
Occupation:	Wife and mother
Destiny:	Salvation

Of course, your life of faith and your list of blessings will differ from Rahab's, but you are indeed a recipient of "every spiritual blessing in the heavenly places in Christ" (Ephesians 1:3). Rejoice!

The Transformation Blessing

It's been a longtime practice of artists to paint over their less impressive works. Sometimes when they do so, they end up creating a grand masterpiece on a canvas that once held a less-than-remarkable picture. Prepare yourself, dear woman of faith, as we view just such a canvas in God's Hebrews 11 portrait gallery. It's His picture of Rahab. As we look intently at Rahab's portrait, we see that hers is a picture on a picture, a "before-and-after" composition:

- *A harlot*—Our now-shining Rahab is a woman with a past that isn't pretty! Making her living and providing for her family in the worst of ways, Rahab is referred to as Rahab-the-harlot.

- *A heroine*—Rahab hid Joshua's spies from her king, saved their lives by sending them out of town a secret way, declared her faith in their God, marked her home with a scarlet cord, and, trusting Joshua's word, waited for his army to return and counted on his mercy toward her. These many acts of faith made Rahab a heroine to the people of Israel. Furthermore, "by faith the harlot Rahab did not perish with those who did not believe, when she had received the spies with peace" (Hebrews 11:31).

🐍 *A hallowed vessel*—Believing in the holy and mighty God of Israel transformed Rahab into a hallowed and holy vessel fit for God's use, giving her a heart of faith and compelling her to act in faith. What the prophet promised became true of Rahab—"Though your sins are like scarlet, they shall be as white as snow; though they are red like crimson, they shall be as wool" (Isaiah 1:18).

Your remarkable transformation—Think about Rahab's life and yours. Do you consider your life to be permanently tainted by past failures, poor decisions, or sickening sin? If so, enjoy the cleansing that is yours through faith in the only One who can wash away your sins. Declare along with Rahab that "the LORD...God, He is God in heaven above and on earth beneath" (Joshua 2:11) and allow Him to wash your crimson sins as white as snow. Let the Lord transform your life, your "before" picture, into something lovely and hallowed, something worthy to hang in the halls of heaven!

I know we've noted it before, but do you recall that only three women are included in God's honor roll of Old Testament saints found in Hebrews 11?[3] Standing tall in this lineup—with Sarah, the mother of faith, and Jochebed, Moses' faithful mother—is Rahab.

— Sarah was married to Abraham, the friend of God (James 2:23).

— Jochebed was married to Amram, of the house of Levi, in the line of Abraham, Isaac, and Jacob (Exodus 2:1).

— Rahab wasn't married at all, but was a harlot, a pagan prostitute.

You can't help but notice that there is one glaring, and even shocking, difference in the lives of Sarah and Jochebed and Rahab. Rahab was Rahab-the-*harlot!* But don't fail to also notice that, through faith, all glaring and shocking differences were obliterated, and these three women stand together equally as remarkable women of faith.

∼ *Rahab's Message for Your Life Today* ∼

There's no way to miss the obvious: *Faith* is Rahab's dominant message. Faith was the starting point for Rahab, and, dear sister, faith is the starting point for you and me as well. But Rahab's life also portrays another strong message—the message of *hope*. Rahab's *hopeless* life gave way to *hopefulness* as she joined God's people in the Promised Land.

And still there are other messages beyond faith and hope from Rahab's remarkable life. Here are a few others for you to hear and heed:

—Hear the Word of the Lord...and believe it!

—Devote yourself to helping God's people.

—Be willing to risk your life for what you believe.

—Devote yourself to your family.

—Wait patiently and trust the Lord wholeheartedly.

—Accept and enjoy God's forgiveness of your sin.

—Bask in God's remarkable grace.

Deborah

~

Remarkable Wisdom

The Path to Greatness

"Deborah...was judging Israel."
JUDGES 4:4
~

*O*ne of the treasures my father passed on to me is a strand of pearls that graced my mother's neck for as many decades as I can remember. They were beautiful then on her, and they are beautiful now as I preserve them for the next generation (Lord willing!). To think that each and every pearl included in my mother's necklace was dived for, harvested, opened, sorted, selected, and then carefully laced into what is now an exquisite heirloom, astounds me.

And, dear reader, that's how I feel as you and I stand on the threshold of gazing at the remarkable Deborah.

A Remarkable Woman

Remarkable! There is no other word to describe the life, ministry, and greatness of Deborah. Hers was truly an uncommon and extraordinary existence. First let's admire the "strand" of her greatness. Then we'll consider each "pearl" that comprised the remarkable beauty of Deborah. Several things make her stand out so dramatically.

- ℘ *A remarkable woman*—The book of Judges introduces Deborah as a prophetess, a wife, and a judge. We also learn that Deborah went out to war with the Israelite army, sang her own song to the Lord (Judges 5:1), and was called "a mother in Israel" (verse 7). No other woman in the Bible is described by such titles.

- ℘ *A remarkable calling*—Deborah is referred to as "a prophetess." Only a handful of women in the Bible have been called to this lofty position.

- ℘ *A remarkable wife*—Despite the unique roles God called Deborah to fulfill for His people, she is also described as "the wife of Lappidoth." Deborah's training ground for remarkable leadership had included time at the hearth where she served as a wife.

- ℘ *A remarkable leader*—Deborah served not only in her home, but also as one of God's judges over His people. Her wise leadership extended beyond her place of judgment—"the palm tree of Deborah"—to the plain of the battlefield where she was shoulder-to-shoulder with Barak, the commander of the army.

- ℘ *A remarkable faith*—Although others wavered— including the warrior Barak—Deborah's faith in God's sure victory over His enemies did not falter, even when the odds were greatly against Israel.

- ℘ *A remarkable poet*—Inspired by God and speaking from a heart of gratitude, Deborah sang! She lifted her spirit and her verses to the heavenly gates as she offered her musical tribute to God for His great victory (Judges 5).

Remarkable! Do you, too, want this rich word to describe your life? While the specifics will differ, your commitment to God and your heart attitude can match Deborah's. How? Just a quick glimpse at her life creates a to-do list (or should we call it a to-be list?). The path to greatness requires you to…be diligent. Be devoted. Be dedicated. Be available. Be prepared. And then, dear one, the rest is up to God!

A Remarkable Wife

When God introduces us to Deborah, He introduces her as "Deborah…the wife of Lappidoth" (Judges 4:4). Oh, Deborah was a prophetess and a judge, but she was also a wife. While nothing is known about Deborah's husband, she was known as his wife.

God used Deborah so mightily on behalf of His people because she was a woman who loved God. As such, we can assume that she obeyed God's Word and followed His guidelines for her as a wife. We've noted these guidelines before, but a quick overview and a fresh reminder never hurts!

> *A wife is to help her husband.* "And the LORD God said, 'It is not good that man should be alone; I will make him a helper comparable to him'" (Genesis 2:18).

> *A wife is to follow her husband.* "Wives, submit [subordinate yourselves, learn to adapt yourselves] to your own husbands, as to the Lord" (Ephesians 5:22).

> *A wife is to respect her husband.* "Let the wife see that she respects [praises and honors] her husband" (Ephesians 5:33).

> *A wife is to love her husband.* "Admonish the young women to love [to be affectionate to] their husbands" (Titus 2:4).

As some wise person reminds us, "God has no greater ground for those who are unfaithful where they are." To become like Deborah—a remarkably wise woman used powerfully by God, a woman given a great ground for service to the kingdom—you must seek to be a remarkable wife. After all, God is honored when you help, follow, respect, and love your husband (Titus 2:5)!

A Remarkable Witness

Visit any art museum, look at any painting there, and you will see that the background sets off the subject and gives the painting its impact. As we admire Deborah, we can't help but notice the background against which her dazzling life is lived out. Exactly what does the path to greatness look like?

> ♪ *The period*—"In those days there was no king in Israel; everyone did what was right in his own eyes" (Judges 21:25). These words paint the background of the book of Judges. Clearly, it was a bleak…and black!…time for Israel, a time characterized by disobedience, idolatry, and defeat. Israel had entered the Promised Land, but because of the many pagan strongholds that remained, the Israelites suffered spiritual decline and the ever-present threat of battle.

> ♪ *The problem*—During these turbulent times, God allowed the children of Israel to fall into the hands of Jabin, the king of Canaan, who harshly oppressed the Israelites for 20 years.

> ♪ *The prophetess*—God's solution to Israel's problem was Deborah, and "the children of Israel came up to her for judgment" (Judges 4:5). She became His witness, His prophetess. As such, Deborah discerned and declared the mind of God. She ministered as a mediator between God and His people. Inspired by God to speak for Him, she poured out His wisdom, knowledge, and instruction when the people came to her for help.

> ♪ *The purpose*—God's purpose in using Deborah as a judge was to lead His people into successful battle

against the Canaanites and ignite spiritual revival in their hearts. Hearing God's Word from and through Deborah awakened God's people to their sagging spiritual condition and stirred up their hearts. As God's witness, Deborah was used by the Lord to bring the Israelites back to Him.

You, too, live in spiritually dark times. Throughout the world, people need God. Make it your aim to follow in the footsteps of Deborah, a remarkable witness. First faithfully and regularly open God's Word so that your own heart is encouraged. And then turn around and spur on another's faith.

Remarkable Wisdom

"Wisdom is oftentimes nearer when we stoop than when we soar." These words of English poet William Wordsworth perfectly describe a key to the fame and success of Deborah, the only female judge of Israel. Exactly how did Deborah's remarkable wisdom exhibit itself? In a word, through her *humility*. Take, for instance, these characteristics of her life.

Deborah did not seek to be a judge—The judges of God's people—including Deborah—were not self-appointed. Instead they were "raised up" by God Himself (Judges 2:16) to administer the laws of the Lord and help deliver His people from their enemies.

Deborah did not seek to lead the people—When times were tough and Israel suffered at the hands of the king of Canaan, Deborah sent for Barak, told him to deploy troops, and shared with him God's promise: "I will deliver him into your hand" (Judges 4:7).

Deborah warned Barak about the consequences of her going into war with him. Despite God's promise of sure victory, Barak refused to go to battle without Deborah. Reluctant to do so, Deborah explained that if she were present, "there will be no glory for you...for the LORD will sell Sisera into the hand of a woman" (verse 9).

Deborah went up with Barak to support him and God's people—Ever the patriot, Deborah declared, "I will surely go with you" (verse 9). Only after calling upon a male leader and then advising him of the consequences of her presence on the battlefield did Deborah go to the front lines.

Don't you agree Deborah definitely shows us the way of wisdom? She truly lived out the adage that the way up is down. The path to greatness in God's kingdom is the path of humble service. Never seeking, never aggressive, never too assertive, Deborah waited on God, encouraged others to take the lead, and assisted only when needed. What would God's advice be to you and me? Remarkable wisdom calls us to...

> be submissive to one another, and be clothed with humility (1 Peter 5:5).

> humble yourself under the mighty hand of God, that He may exalt you in due time (1 Peter 5:6).

A Remarkable Warrior

God asks the question, "Who can find a virtuous woman?" (Proverbs 31:10 KJV). Well, in Deborah He has found one! A virtuous woman is a woman who possesses power of mind (moral principles and attitudes) and power of body (ability and effectiveness).

Deborah, a great judge in Israel, had both. Strong in mind and morals, Deborah administered God's law and wisely managed and counseled His people. And strong in body, "Deborah arose and went with Barak" to war (Judges 4:9). Deborah called upon her complete store of mental toughness and physical energy. Such toughness and energy are the primary traits of a successful army, and they also characterize Deborah, God's prophetess and remarkable warrior! And beloved, please note—God has nothing but praise for this remarkable woman and warrior (Judges 4–5).

Don't you, too, desire to be identified by God (and others) as a virtuous woman? The day-in, day-out duties you encounter call for you to possess a significant store of power of mind and body. Mental toughness and physical energy will keep you from giving up, giving in, dropping out, or quitting short of God's goal for you as you, like Deborah, serve as His remarkable warrior even on the homefront! You, too, can (and must!) move through the challenges and duties of life with valor, courage, stamina, endurance, and power—*His* power.

A Remarkable Writer

I love being a writer! And I put both computer and pen to use in the process. But how did one chronicle important events in a day and age when the instruments and media for writing were cumbersome and crude?

This was the predicament Deborah, the prophetess and judge over God's people, found herself in. The important event was God's victory over Israel's enemies (Judges 4:23). The day and age was a time when the law of Moses was still being written on stones (Joshua 8:32). Yet, when God "fought from the heavens" and "the stars from their courses fought against" Israel's adversaries (Judges 5:20), Deborah's full heart yearned to keep the memory alive forever. So how did she do that?

Deborah sang! Deborah not only had "a sword in her hand," but she also had "a song in her heart." Just as Moses and Miriam and David (Exodus 15 and 2 Samuel 22) sang after God's mighty conquests, Deborah sang too, detailing God's triumph over His foes. Judges 5 contains Deborah's poem of praise. Deborah, the writer, gave testimony to God and praised Him in song for...

—marching against the opposing armies,

—His righteous acts, and

—acting on Deborah's behalf.

Jesus tells us that "out of the abundance of the heart" the mouth speaks, and "a good man out of the good treasure of his heart brings forth good" (Luke 6:45). Clearly, Deborah's song spilled forth from a heart filled with "good treasure." Her song reveals all that was in her heart—the worship and reverence, the honor and love, the joy and exultation, the praise and adoration. Deborah was a woman after God's own heart. Hers was a heart "steadfast, trusting in the LORD" (Psalm 112:7).

What is in your heart, dear one? If you were to sing unto the Lord, what words would you put to the song of your heart? Consider these remarkable "writing guidelines" from Scripture:

> Let the words of my mouth and the meditation of my heart be acceptable in Your sight (Psalm 19:14).

> [Speak] to one another in psalms and hymns and spiritual songs, singing and making melody in your heart to the Lord (Ephesians 5:19).

∼ Deborah's Message for Your Life Today ∼

As the woman dubbed by God as "a mother in Israel" (Judges 5:7), the remarkable Deborah has much to say to you and me! Her role among God's people was that of leader, judge, warrior, motivator, deliverer, and protector. (Could you use help in any of these familiar roles as you live out God's plan for your life?) Pause now and give thought to a few of the factors that foster a life of great faith, deep commitment, excellent wisdom, and abundant spiritual energy:

> *A life spent in God's Word*—All Scripture is profitable for instruction in righteousness, and God's Word thoroughly—*thoroughly!*—equips you to be a Deborah, a woman of remarkable wisdom, and to sustain a lifetime of good works (2 Timothy 3:16-17).

> *A life spent in prayer*—Do you want to do great things *for* God? Then ask great things *of* God. Scripture says, "You do not have because you do not ask" (James 4:2). So ask for greater strength and perseverance, greater faith, wisdom, and devotion. These are all needed on the path to greatness. Deborah needed all of the above, and you will too!

> *A life spent in obedience*—As you dedicate your life to being "a doer of the word," God promises that you will be blessed in all you do (James 1:22,25). Like Deborah, a woman with a heart in tune with God's Word and with a heart of obedience that heeded God's Word, you will be blessed…and so will others.

Ruth
and
Naomi

~

Remarkable
Devotion

Enduring Difficult Times

> *"The woman survived her two sons
> and her husband."*
> RUTH 1:5
> ~

uring my years as an English literature teacher, it was amazing to discover that no student had trouble remembering the famous opening words of Charles Dickens' *A Tale of Two Cities*. You probably know them too: "It was the best of times, it was the worst of times." Well, dear reader, these familiar words also aptly describe ten years of the life of a woman named Naomi. Let's see how. And as you read the two chapters that shine the spotlight on two women of remarkable devotion—devotion to God and to one another—keep in mind that their lives are so entwined that it is impossible to think of (or read about) one without touching upon the life of the other.

The Seasons of a Woman's Life

"It was the best of times"—Naomi and her family, made up of her husband, Elimelech, and their two sons, Mahlon and

Chilion, left their hometown of Bethlehem. Because of famine in Judah, the family settled in Moab where there was food (Ruth 1:1). Yes, times there were good. They feasted while those in their homeland endured famine. It was a season of plenty. And Naomi's family expanded when her two sons were married. Each had met his mate in Moab (verse 4). Those days had truly been sweet!

"It was the worst of times"—But soon the death knell sounded. First, Naomi's beloved husband died, and then she lost her two precious sons (verses 3 and 5). It was a triple blow to the heart and the life of this wife and mother as a dark season dawned. How could something that had been so good turn so sour? Naomi seemed alone in the world except for her sons' wives.

Your times—Dear one, have you ever felt like Naomi must have felt? Have you ever moved into what was supposed to be an ideal future, experienced a season of bliss and blessing, and then faced a season of great loss and pain? Please take these two strong promises of the Lord to heart as the seasons of your life alter and you must endure difficult times:

> For I know the thoughts that I think toward you, says the Lord, thoughts of peace and not of evil, to give you a future and a hope (Jeremiah 29:11).

> And we know that all things work together for good to those who love God, to those who are the called according to His purpose (Romans 8:28).

How does one endure difficult times? By clinging to the One who made these promises. Like Naomi, you can walk the path of "a future and a hope" as you trust the Lord that your trail of tears will lead you straight into the discovery of the good, acceptable, and perfect will of God (Romans 12:2)!

Coping with Tragedy

Our Naomi definitely faced extremely difficult times! But she teaches you and me how to cope with tragedy. Over coffee (wouldn't that be wonderful!), we can be sure Naomi would say, "When you are in a hard place in life, it is not the time to collapse, to cave in, to fall apart, or to break down. It is time to trust God."

When her life caved in, Naomi, a woman who was devoted to God, began learning how to trust God more. Amazingly, she heard news that the Lord had once again given bread to His people in Bethlehem. So the bereft Naomi, the woman who "went out full" (Ruth 1:21) from Bethlehem oh-so-many-years-ago, left the foreign land of Moab to return to the land of Judah. But it was a long road home, and much happened between Point A (Moab) and Point B (Bethlehem)! There was much to trust the Lord for as "she went out from the place where she was" (verse 7). Note these stops—and changes—along the way:

- Naomi's two daughters-in-law started out with her.

- Naomi urged these two young widows to return, each to their mother's house.

- Naomi kissed the two women goodbye.

- Naomi's daughter-in-law Orpah returned to her home.

- Naomi's daughter-in-law Ruth stayed with Naomi (verses 6-19).

Certainly this was not how Naomi had expected her life to unfold, but she was learning to trust God more, to trust Him to work in her life through unexpected people, tragic events, and difficult circumstances.

The people? Where once Naomi had depended upon her husband and sons, now she was to depend upon Ruth, one lone, young, and widowed daughter-in-law.

The events? Certainly Naomi would have chosen to have God work through the lives of her menfolk, but she was now trusting Him to work through the tragedy of their deaths.

The circumstances? Never had Naomi imagined that she would be going back to Bethlehem without her husband or sons, but she was headed in that direction. It was a long road home. She would have to trust God. There was no other way to cope with her tragedy.

Going Home

All the world loves a reunion! Relatives from far away regularly gather for family reunions. Best friends rendezvous to catch up on each other's lives. Military squadrons meet and renew their wartime friendships. High schools and colleges host get-togethers and homecoming events so graduates can stay in touch.

A different kind of reunion, however, took place thousands of years ago. It was not by choice. It was not for pleasure. And it was not with joyful anticipation. Instead, it was by necessity. You see, Naomi was going home. As we've learned, Naomi was formerly of Bethlehem. She had left that town with her husband and children, perhaps full of dreams of a splendid future. But her dreams had turned to disaster. Naomi's husband and both her children had died. Even one of her daughters-in-law had chosen to remain behind. So Naomi was returning to Bethlehem…as a widow…with only Ruth, a devoted daughter-in-law from a foreign land. In Naomi's own words, she was going home "empty."

Naomi, whose name means "pleasant," along with Ruth, walked 70 dusty miles back home to Bethlehem (verse 19). As her former friends greeted her with, "Is this Naomi?" she could only reply, "Do not call me Naomi; call me Mara [Mara means "bitter"]....I went out full, and the LORD has brought me home again empty" (verse 21).

God works in our lives through people, events, and circumstances. But we must also note (and agree), that God never means to make us bitter—only to make us better! Now the question is, What can we do to "be fruitful in the land of [our] affliction" (Genesis 41:52)?

> *Remember these promises*—God's thoughts toward you are thoughts of peace and not of evil, to give you a future and a hope (Jeremiah 29:11), and you can know that all things work together for your good (Romans 8:28).
>
> *Give thanks always*—It is impossible to be bitter and thankful at the same time (Ephesians 5:20).
>
> *Pray without ceasing*—Even through tears, prayer is the heart's song to God (1 Thessalonians 5:17).
>
> *Reach out to others*—Comfort others with the comfort God has given you (2 Corinthians 1:4).

"Happenstance"

I hear it all the time, and I'm sure you do too: "It was a coincidence!" But, dear one, there is no such thing in the life of God's children as happenstance or coincidence. There is only the great sovereignty of God Almighty, who watches over His children and guides their steps, sometimes quite obviously...and other times not so obviously. Well, God's sovereignty was at work in Ruth's life during her difficult times on one particular day that "happened" to go like this...

Bethlehem was the place. Food was the pressing need. A field of grain was the setting. Ruth was the woman, and she "happened to come to the part of the field belonging to Boaz, who was of the family of Elimelech" (Ruth 2:3). Our Ruth ventured out in search of grain for daily bread—and just happened to end up in the field that belonged to the man Boaz...who just happened to be related to her by marriage. Going out to gather grain in her new homeland, Ruth was without a guide, without a companion. She was on her own. She was alone...except for God, who directed her steps to one particular field, owned by one particular relative. Beloved, to fast-forward in our story, Boaz later becomes Ruth's husband (Ruth 4:13)!

We'll look at the details of this remarkable "turn of events" later. But for now, marvel at God's watch-care, His leading, guidance, and provision for His child Ruth. As you consider these "happenstances" in Ruth's life, ponder these words by seventeenth-century writer and minister Matthew Henry:

> God wisely orders small events; and those that seem altogether...[conditional] serve his own glory and the good of his people. Many a great affair is brought about by a little turn, which seemed... [lucky or accidental] to us, but was directed by Providence with design.[1]

Every woman of God experiences difficult times. But there is a way for you and me to endure such times. How? We must seek to see the hand of God in all of the events, the coincidences, the chance happenings, the luck and flukes of life. If we believe in a sovereign God, if we believe in His loving providence, then we must choose to consider all that touches our lives as Him at work once again. So, dear one, we must learn to...

Look for the hand of God.

Believe that God works in our lives, in all that we encounter and all that we experience.

Trust that God works *all things* together for our ultimate good (Romans 8:28).

Under His Wings

Yes, times were hard and difficult for Naomi and Ruth. Yet God was ever-present, ever-faithful, and ever-at-work in the details of their daily lives. Although their days were dark, the tiny book of Ruth surprisingly includes a pair of heartfelt hymns beautifully sung by two people who took refuge under the wings of God.

Ruth's Hymn

A woman devoted to God, Ruth was also devoted to Naomi. Although raised in the pagan nation of Moab, Ruth gave her heart and allegiance to Naomi's God, the God of Israel, the one true God. In her faith-filled declaration to Naomi, her bereaved mother-in-law, Ruth uttered words of remarkable devotion that read like a hymn.

> Wherever you go, I will go;
>
> And wherever you lodge, I will lodge;
>
> Your people shall be my people,
>
> And your God, my God.
>
> Where you die, I will die,
>
> And there will I be buried
>
> (Ruth 1:16-17).

Boaz's Hymn

Boaz, too, was devoted to God. He was also a landowner and a distant relative of Ruth through her dead husband's father. Upon meeting Ruth, he blessed and encouraged her in her newfound faith in God with words that also sound like a hymn:

> The LORD repay your work, and
> a full reward be given you
> by the LORD God of Israel,
> under whose wings you have come
>> for refuge
> (Ruth 2:12).

What beautiful words! Perhaps Boaz saw the struggling Ruth—a woman who "happened" to wander into his field and labored so diligently in the hot barley fields to gather one more day's worth of food for herself and her widowed mother-in-law—as a fragile baby chick. His song pictures Ruth as finding refuge under God's wings—His wings of protection and safety, wings of care, strength, and warmth. In the Holy Scriptures, God is indeed portrayed as a mother bird who shelters her young with her wings (Psalm 36:7). And Boaz uses this metaphor to bless one who has placed remarkable trust in God and found refuge there.

Naomi trusted in God. Ruth depended upon God. And Boaz relied on God.

And now for you. Do *you* trust in God and God alone? Do you depend totally on the One who protects and provides for His own? Are you resting under His wings of love? Dear fellow sufferer, *God*, your heavenly Father, is responsible for protecting you. *Your* responsibility is to trust in Him and to rest under the shadow of His wings.

∾ Ruth and Naomi's Message for Your Life Today ∾

Beloved, you and I must be ever learning from "older women"—both those in the Bible and those in our everyday lives—who have gone before us, who have forged ahead in life, who pave the way, show us the way, and teach us God's way for managing life (Titus 2:3). I believe the following just might reflect a checklist for enduring difficult times, taught by two of God's remarkable women of the Bible—Naomi and Ruth. And then, as a treat, enjoy the lyrics of a favorite old hymn, appropriately entitled "Under His Wings."

- ♪ Things change...but God doesn't.

- ♪ Suffering is a "given" in life (John 16:33).

- ♪ God works in your life through people, events, circumstances...and even "happenstance"!

- ♪ When suffering comes, seek and plan to respond in a godly, faith-filled way, in the strength of the Lord.

- ♪ Believe in the promises of God and draw upon their truth, comfort, and strength.

- ♪ Be sure your song rises above your sorrow.

- ♪ Realize you may rest at any time and at all times under the wings of God.

Under His Wings

"Hide me under the shadow of Your wings."
(Psalm 17:8)

Under His wings I am safely abiding,
Though the night deepens and tempests are wild;
Still I can trust Him; I know He will keep me,
He has redeemed me, and I am His child.

Under His wings, what a refuge in sorrow!
How the heart yearningly turns to His rest!
Often when earth has no balm for my healing,
There I find comfort, and there I am blessed.

Under His wings, O what precious enjoyment!
There will I hide till life's trials are o'er;
Sheltered, protected, no evil can harm me,
Resting in Jesus, I'm safe evermore.

Under His wings, under His wings,
Who from His love can sever?
Under His wings my soul shall abide,
Safely abide forever.[2]

Enjoying
God's Blessings

*"Blessed be he of the LORD, who has not forsaken
His kindness to the living and the dead!"*

RUTH 2:20

≈

What would you do if...
   ...you were a widow,
      ...your sons had died,
         ...your daughter-in-law was your only companion,
         ...you needed food?

This was exactly the predicament Naomi found herself in after she returned to Bethlehem with Ruth, her daughter-in-law (Ruth 1:22). Too old to labor herself, Naomi had to depend solely on Ruth for the basics of life. Times were hard when Ruth gleaned barley from the harvested fields. The law of Moses stipulated that any grain dropped by the reapers as they brought in their crops could be gleaned by the poor (Leviticus 23:22). This law was tailor-made for those like Naomi and Ruth...a blessing from God! But there's more!

The Kindness of the Lord

Beyond this law, the kindness of the Lord was at work in other ways. Unknowingly, Ruth "happened"—by God's sovereign design—into the field of a relative named Boaz. This man then took on the support of both Ruth and Naomi by giving Ruth extended privileges in the reaping of his fields along with extra food, extra grain, and protection.

When Ruth reported to Naomi these acts of kindness from Boaz, Naomi's heart warmed for the first time in many months. Hope and joy began to push their way up through the bitter, hard crust that encased Naomi's once-happy heart. Her mouth opened to offer the praise, "Blessed be he of the LORD, who has not forsaken His kindness to the living and the dead!" (Ruth 2:20). In Naomi's cold heart there appeared a glimmer of understanding of God's sovereign working in her life, of His steadfast lovingkindness, and of His mercy being showered on them through Boaz.

Love for One Another

Everyone wonders at what happened next in the lives of our two brave, devoted-to-one-another women. The scene appears as quite puzzling, even questionable, yet it was another way God was at work and actively blessing Ruth and Naomi. We have very little knowledge of the customs in the small town in Israel where Ruth and Naomi lived, but Ruth, chapter 3, gives us some interesting clues. Follow along. And as you consider the actions of this mother- and daughter-in-law, don't fail to notice how they loved one another, looked out for one another, and sought the best for one another.

Naomi wanted the best for Ruth. Naomi noticed the budding respect between Ruth and Boaz and obviously saw a hopeful future for Ruth as a married woman. Therefore, this older, wiser woman coached the younger in the customs of her land—customs for securing a marriage partner. Naomi told Ruth...

...how to look ("wash yourself and anoint yourself, put on your best garment") and

...how to act ("when he lies down...uncover his feet and lie down...and he will tell you what you should do").

And Ruth wanted the best for Naomi. By now Ruth knew that Boaz could—and wanted to—provide for the aged and needy Naomi (Ruth 2:16; 3:16). Ruth, too, wanted that security for Naomi. Therefore, the younger woman obediently followed through on Naomi's instructions to propose marriage to Boaz. She said, "All that you say to me I will do" (Ruth 3:5).

Naomi and Ruth offer us a matched set of beautiful portraits of selflessness. Each clearly wanted what was best for the other. But...what about you? What sort of picture are you painting with your life? Are you truly loving other people? Do you desire what is best for others? Pray today for a more generous, self-less attitude toward others—even your in-laws!

A Virtuous Woman

To update our progress, remember that Ruth was not from Israel; she was a Moabite. Ruth was not Jewish; she was a pagan. Ruth had no husband; she was a widow. Yet Ruth left her homeland, her family, and her religion to follow Naomi back to Bethlehem. Everyone there saw in Ruth's hard work her concern for her widowed mother-in-law (Ruth 2:11). As the landowner Boaz declared to Ruth, "All the people of my town know that you are a virtuous woman" (Ruth 3:11).

The word *virtuous* describes both Ruth (Ruth 3:11) and the wife of Proverbs 31:10-31. With amazing parallel, they share at least eight character traits. Each woman was...

1. Devoted to her family (Ruth 1:15-18/Proverbs 31:10-12,23)

2. Delighting in her work (Ruth 2:2/Proverbs 31:13)

3. Diligent in her labor (Ruth 2:7,17,23/Proverbs 31:14-18,19-21,24,27)

4. Dedicated to godly speech (Ruth 2:10,13/Proverbs 31:26)

5. Dependent on God (Ruth 2:12/Proverbs 31:25b,30)

6. Dressed with care (Ruth 3:3/Proverbs 31:22,25a)

7. Discreet with men (Ruth 3:6-13/Proverbs 31:11-12,23)

8. Delivering blessings (Ruth 4:14,15/Proverbs 31:28,29,31)[1]

Pray now and ask God to work each of these godly virtues into your heart and life, that all the people of your town would see that you, too, are a virtuous woman!

A Virtuous Man

Both Ruth and the Proverbs 31 woman were "virtuous" women. But did you know that the book of Ruth also details the qualities of a virtuous man? The man was Boaz, the hard-working landowner who became Ruth's husband. Note God's list of the virtues exhibited by Boaz's sterling life. He was...

> *Diligent*—Boaz is described as "a man of great wealth" (Ruth 2:1), and we see him carefully and thoughtfully overseeing his property.

> *Friendly*—Boaz greeted his workers with warmth, and even welcomed the stranger named Ruth (2:4,8).

> *Merciful*—Noticing Ruth at work, Boaz asked about her situation and acted on her behalf (2:7).

> *Godly*—Boaz asked Jehovah to bless Ruth in return for her care for Naomi (2:12).

❧ *Encouraging*—Boaz pointed out Ruth's strong qualities and spoke of them to cheer her on (2:12; 3:11).

❧ *Generous*—Although Ruth needed food and was willing to work for it, Boaz gave her extra (2:15).

❧ *Kind*—When Ruth reported the considerate ways of Boaz, Naomi thanked God for His kindness shown to both of them through Boaz (2:20).

❧ *Discreet*—Boaz exhibited wise discretion by sending Ruth home before daylight (3:14).

❧ *Faithful*—Following through on his promise to Ruth, Boaz "went to court" to clear the way to marry her (4:1).[2]

Are you single? Look for these qualities in the man you may seek to marry. Don't settle for less than a virtuous man who is godly, diligent, faithful…(you know the list!).

Are you married? Remember to prize, praise, and pray for these qualities in your beloved husband.

Are you a mother? Be sure to instill these qualities in the hearts and minds of your daughters (your young Ruths) and your sons (your young Boazes). Point your children to God's high standards and teach them to embrace His ways as their own. Train each son to be a virtuous man and each daughter to appreciate men who possess godly virtues.

A Grandmother's Heart

As the grandmother of five little ones under four years old, I can't resist adding this section. As we've witnessed, during her life Naomi traveled from a mountaintop existence of bliss into a deep and dark valley of sorrow. But blessed be the Lord! He did not leave Naomi in her valley of despair, hopelessness, and emptiness. God blessed Naomi with a grandchild, a grandson, and she knew happiness again. How she must have welcomed the warmth of fresh-flowing love and life as she "took the child and...became a nurse to him" (Ruth 4:16) and as God began to grow in her the heart of a grandmother. What did the arrival of tiny Obed signify to Naomi as she held him in her arms?

- A continuation of the heritage of her dead husband (Ruth 4:17).

- A person to love since losing her own two sons (verse 15).

- A child to care for and serve as a nursemaid for.

- An offspring who would help care for Naomi in her old age.

- A "restorer of life" and a hope for the future!

The role of grandmother is a great privilege God grants women. (And when you talk to a grandmother, be prepared for glowing tales and a plethora of photographs!) But being a grandmother also gives such blessed women new opportunities, challenges, and responsibilities. The heart of a godly grandmother is dedicated to the practices listed below. If you're a grandmother, are you living out the "grand"? If you're not a grandmother, pray for your own dear grandmother.

Give a godly example.
Remember important occasions.
Always love your grandchildren's parents—no matter what!
Never show favoritism.
Develop a personal relationship with each grandchild.

Stars in Her Crown

Do you hear wedding bells? Proverbs 12:4 proclaims, "A virtuous woman is a crown to her husband" (KJV). And our Ruth was such a woman of virtuous character. She married a man named Boaz, a man of virtuous character. It was a grand day when they married one another!

But hang on! The union of this noble couple continued a line of descendants who loved God. Through their marriage a wonderful, godly lineage extended through time and for eternity, and each offspring became another star in Ruth's (and Naomi's) crown of virtue. Take a moment to admire these gems in Ruth and Boaz's genealogy. "Now this is the genealogy of... Boaz" (Ruth 4:18,21).

"Boaz begot Obed"—As one Bible scholar has noted, "Through the birth of Obed, God wove the thread of Ruth's life most intricately into the web of the history of His people. She became the chosen line through which later the Savior of the world appeared."[3]

"Obed begot Jesse"—Just as Isaiah had prophesied, "There shall come forth a Rod from the stem of Jesse, and a Branch shall grow out of his roots" (Isaiah 11:1). Beloved, that Rod and that Branch was the Lord Jesus Christ.

"Jesse begot David"—The hope of a messianic king and kingdom was fulfilled in the Lord Jesus Christ through the lineage of David, his father Jesse, and his grandfather Obed, who was born to Boaz and Ruth.

Jesus Christ—The family tree or "the book of the genealogy of Jesus Christ, the Son of David" includes these names: Boaz, Obed, Jesse, and David (Matthew 1:1,5-6).

Do you have children or grandchildren? If you do, they are precious treasures, stars in your crown, blessings from God. Pray for them—fervently! Encourage them in the Lord—mightily! Ensure that they know about Jesus—abundantly! Support their spiritual growth—heartily!

~ Ruth and Naomi's Message for Your Life Today ~

As we look back over the tiny book of Ruth, we can only wonder at God's gracious dealings and abundant blessings poured out upon the two needy widows, Naomi and Ruth, who in turn poured out to others. From them we immediately receive many messages—

Both suffered death and loss.	Naomi counseled Ruth.
Both believed in God.	Ruth shared tiny Obed.
Both loved the other.	Naomi helped with Obed.
Ruth worked the fields.	

- *Message 1:* Look for the kindness of the Lord extended to you through the good deeds of others.
- *Message 2:* Extend the kindness of the Lord to others through your own good deeds.

Here's a thought to tape over the kitchen sink, stick on the refrigerator door, attach to your computer, and affix to your bathroom mirror:

~ True service is love in working clothes ~

Both Ruth and Naomi were women of many virtues. But perhaps their most outstanding distinction was the servant heart each possessed. They consistently ministered to one another. And like these two remarkable women, you can put on the work clothes of love and engage in...

Service to others—It all begins with a decision to serve others—anyone and everyone. And Jesus models this heart attitude for us, for He "did not come to be served, but to serve" (Matthew 20:28).

Service to your husband—God's Word is clear: "Whatever you do [including serving your husband], do it heartily, as to the Lord and not to men" (Colossians 3:23).

Service to your children—As a familiar kitchen plaque reads, "Divine services rendered here three times a day!" It's true that not only every meal prepared, but also every piece of clothing washed, every room tidied, every floor swept, every ride given is love in action.

Service to your church—Married or single, you can exercise your servant-heart at your church. There are always meals to take to those in need, pew racks to stock, chairs to set up, and Sunday school classes to teach.

Service to all—The New Testament points out the service rendered by the godly women who gave strangers a place to stay, washed the saints' feet, relieved the afflicted, and diligently performed good works (1 Timothy 5:10). May you join their inspiring ranks! May yours be the heart of a servant. May you pass on God's blessings to others.

Hannah

~

Remarkable Sacrifice

A Weaving of Grace

Hannah "prayed to the LORD."
1 SAMUEL 1:10

*I*f you've ever attended church on Mother's Day, you know that the story of Hannah's life and the virtues of this remarkable woman and mother of the Bible is a favorite subject. We have much to learn from dear Hannah about God's grace in unpleasant circumstances and about the beauty of faith and sacrifice.

So I invite you to get ready to meet one of the most gracious women in the Bible. Even her very name—*Hannah*—means "gracious, graciousness, grace, and favor." Hannah is one of the few women in the sacred Scriptures about whom nothing negative is reported.

The Divine Weaver

How did Hannah become such a testimony to God's great grace? Short, simple answers to that question include a series of bitter words—words such as difficulty, pain, suffering, sacrifice. For Hannah—and for all women of faith (including you, dear one)—God, "the Divine Weaver," used some dark threads when He wove the rich tapestry of her life.

Before we look closely at the various threads running through Hannah's life, let me share with you the poignant words of this bit of poetry that was given to me by an attendant at a wool factory in Ireland. A copy of the poem was tacked onto the frame of a giant loom containing an exquisite half-finished tapestry. It was aptly entitled...

The Divine Weaver

My life is but a weaving
Between my Lord and me;
I cannot choose the colors
He worketh steadily.

Ofttimes He weaveth sorrow
And I, in foolish pride,
Forget that He seeth the upper,
And I the under side.

Not till the loom is silent
And the shuttles cease to fly,
Shall God unroll the canvas
And explain the reason why.

The dark threads are as needful
In the Weaver's skillful hand,
As the threads of gold and silver
In the pattern He has planned.

Rest assured that the Master Weaver is weaving the threads of your life too, one event at a time, one moment at a time. He alone knows the pattern. Won't you trust Him as He graciously makes an exquisite work of your life?

Threads of Pain

Young girls often dream of someday getting married. They may even spend years imagining and planning the perfect wedding day, honeymoon, and life. In fact, most bridal magazines and books are purchased by young women who don't even have a prospect for marriage! They are simply fantasizing about their future.

If, as a young girl, Hannah had dreamed of the perfect marriage, her dreams were eventually met by a rather harsh reality. Hannah did marry, and her husband's name was Elkanah, a Levite from one of the most honorable families of priests. Hannah's husband may have been a wonderful man, yet there were some not-so-wonderful facts about Hannah's marriage to Elkanah. Those sad details became the dark threads of pain woven throughout Hannah's life.

> ℷ *Painful fact #1: Hannah shared her husband with another woman*—The Bible reports that Hannah's husband "had two wives: the name of one was Hannah" (1 Samuel 1:2). Hannah's name is listed first, indicating that she was probably Elkanah's first wife and that later a second wife was added.

> ℷ *Painful fact #2: Hannah had no children*—Hannah did not receive the blessing of the happy marriage and family she had hoped for. Instead of ringing with the laughter and noise of active children, Hannah's house may have echoed with muffled sobs and tears, for "the LORD had closed her womb" (verse 6).

> ℷ *Painful fact #3: Hannah was harassed by her husband's other wife*—Insult was added to injury for the lovely Hannah. Peninnah, Elkanah's second wife and Hannah's rival, "provoked her severely, to make her miserable" (verse 6).

Dark Threads the Weaver Needs is the title of an insightful book about suffering, and a title that speaks to precious Hannah's life.[1] Does it speak to your life situation too? If so, can you gather together those dark threads of pain and then lay them carefully into the wise and wonderful hand of God? He will use those dark threads to make your life a beautiful masterpiece and testimony to His glory!

Threads of Reverence

Woven into the texture of Hannah's soul alongside the dark thread of pain was the glorious gold thread of reverence for God. Hannah's life was filled with problems, but it was also filled with fervent worship. At the appointed time each year, "she went up to the house of the LORD" (verse 7) with her husband to worship and make sacrifices to God.

Consider what worship is and some of its benefits.

Worship is fellowship with God—We don't know whether Hannah talked to her husband about the relentless aggravation she suffered from his other wife. But we do see that Hannah worshiped God and fellowshipped with Him. Jehovah was definitely One she could tell her troubles to.

Worship is the first step toward wisdom—How do you handle a hard situation? Hannah went to God for wisdom about how to deal with the daily difficulties of her life. As she worshiped, God led her in the path of wisdom—*His* wisdom.

Worship is inward reverence—It's relatively easy to do things for God—to give money, to serve in church, to regularly attend events. But true worship is personal, a matter of the heart rather than external activity.

"Worship quickens the conscience by the holiness of God, feeds the mind with the beauty of God, opens the heart to the love of God, and devotes the will to the purpose of God."[2] Can any other activity be more important!

Dear one, when you suffer—worship! When you are confused—worship! When you are lonely—worship! When you are anxious—worship! When you are criticized—worship!

Make it your daily habit to liberally fill God's hand with the golden threads of your reverential worship. Allow Him to weave an abundance of gold among the darker threads of the tapestry He's making of your life.

A Rope of Prayer

When a tapestry is complete, the weaver hangs it by a cord strong enough to support its weight. For the splendid weaving of Hannah's life, that cord was the rope of prayer. Here's how it came to be.

Hannah's afflictions were many and heavy—so many and so heavy that tears had become her diet as "she wept and did not eat" (1 Samuel 1:7). Bitterness of soul and anguish of heart clouded her spirit. Many people in her place would have given up...or blown up! But Hannah shows us the better way—she "prayed to the LORD" (verse 10). Her soul may have been dark, but her faith was radiant as she knelt down and poured out her distress and disappointment to God in prayer.

The Hebrew language has many words for the act of prayer, but the specific Hebrew term used to describe Hannah's heartfelt prayer in the house of the Lord is *palal*, meaning "to entreat, to make supplication."[3] You see, Hannah pleaded with the Lord in her trouble. She petitioned the Almighty. She made her request known unto God.

Beloved woman of God, take inventory of your life. Hannah had marital problems. Do you? She was denied motherhood—something she sorely desired. What do you long for but have not been given? Provocation, cruelty, and ridicule were part of Hannah's everyday life. Do you regularly suffer any kind of mistreatment?

Suffering from what she did not have, precious Hannah grabbed onto what she did have—the rope of prayer—and drew herself and her situation up to God's heavenly throne. Though weak from sadness and weeping, Hannah found her fingers of faith strong enough to seize her one link to God, and she pulled the rope of prayer.

You can do the same, my friend. And when you do, you can enjoy the benefits of doing so.

Holding onto the rope of prayer helps bring you into the will of God.

Handling the rope of prayer develops strong spiritual muscles.

Hanging onto the rope of prayer in turbulent times gives you an anchor, however rough or long-lasting the storm.

Hitching yourself to God by the rope of prayer moves you along His path for your life.

Threads of Devotion

The threads have been gathered, and the shuttle is flying. God is at work weaving His divine design for Hannah's life. He has included dark threads—the black and charcoal-gray hues of trial—as well as the glittering golden threads of Hannah's worship. We've also noted that the sturdy, powerful rope of prayer securely attaches Hannah to her God. Now, as we hear her speak to God, sterling silver makes its appearance as Hannah utters a vow to her Lord.

To review, terrible tension had been mounting in her home. Hannah's marriage hadn't gone the way she had hoped. Her family life hadn't either—she had borne no children. And her relationship with her husband's other wife was unbearable. Hannah's situation seemed hopeless, as did the situation of her people, the nation of Israel, for "there was no king in Israel; everyone did what was right in his own eyes" (Judges 21:25), and "the word of the LORD was rare" (1 Samuel 3:1).

What happened to God's plan for His chosen people? What about all He promised them? Where were the leaders He said He would provide? God was silent, and His people were lost.

True, a baby would bring joy to Hannah's heart, brighten her life, and silence her critics. But as time—the preordained and perfect timing of God's plan—went on, Hannah's desires slowly grew beyond her personal yearnings and focused instead on God. The time Hannah spent wanting and waiting gave Him time to work in her a most noble desire. Hannah came to desire a man for God, not just for herself. So Hannah vowed, "O LORD of hosts, if You will...give Your maidservant a male child, then I will give him to the LORD all the days of his life" (1 Samuel 1:11).

Here's a challenge: Do you as a woman of faith want what you want for selfish purposes, to "spend it on your pleasures" (James 4:3), or do your desires focus on God and His ultimate purposes? Be sure to take time to evaluate...and adjust...your desires and the motives behind your prayers.

Threads of Faith

At long last Hannah's ordeal was over! After the trials of sharing a husband with another wife, dealing with the heart-breaking inability to have children, being incessantly harassed by the other wife, and even the trial of finding herself misunderstood by the temple priest (1 Samuel 1:14), Hannah suddenly found her misery pushed aside by joy.

What prompted this radical change of emotions? The Scripture tells us that Eli, the priest, gave Hannah this priestly blessing: "Go in peace, and the God of Israel grant your petition which you have asked of Him" (verse 17). Hannah's long wanted and long prayed-for child would be forthcoming!

At this point in the weaving of Hannah's life story, a new color (I imagine the color blue) appears in the tapestry, denoting her confident faith in the Lord—a faith that spanned the blue skies and connected her to her heavenly Father. But note this—nothing in her life had changed! Nevertheless, *Hannah believed,* and so found joy in the promise.

What remarkable faith, indeed! After Eli had pronounced his blessing, this woman who had fasted, wept, and prayed in anguish and bitterness of soul "went her way and ate, and her face was no longer sad" (verse 18). She didn't have a baby— she wasn't even pregnant yet!—but she believed in faith that one day she would have a son.

Beloved woman of God, are heavenly threads of faith woven throughout the warp and woof of your existence? Does your faith, revealed in the everyday events of life, evidence a trust in God that shoots to the heavens? When God speaks to you through His Word, do you believe Him? Do you hold on to the "exceedingly great and precious promises" of God (2 Peter 1:4)? Do you trust what God says, even when nothing about your situation seems to be changing for the better? As a children's song reminds us, "Faith is just believing what God says He will do."

～ Hannah's Message for Your Life Today ～

Hannah's story is far from over! More noble threads of virtue await us in the next chapter. But we simply must pause and let the portion of the remarkable weaving of Hannah's life that we do see make its impression upon our appreciation and upon our souls. As you and I stand side-by-side gazing at what *is* seen of Hannah's humble and humanly unhappy life, there's no doubt that what we view is beautiful! It's remarkable! (How, we wonder, does—and can—God do that!) There's more to come, but for now, mark these mighty messages.

A message of hope—The truth that God works all things together for your good (Romans 8:28) should give your sore heart hope, no matter what is happening to you. The Divine Weaver is in charge of the outcome of your life and is at work overruling all pain, evil, and mistreatment to make your life a weaving of grace—His divine masterpiece.

A message of blessing—Hannah had problems...and Hannah pleaded with the Lord about those problems. She presented her hurting heart and her requests to the God of the impossible. And, dear one, Hannah was blessed. When you pray, God's blessing takes on many forms. You are blessed by peace, *His* peace that passes all understanding (Philippians 4:7). You are blessed by comfort, the comfort that comes from "the Father of mercies and the God of all comfort" (2 Corinthians 1:3). While you may not receive that for which you ask, you are most definitely blessed spiritually "with every spiritual blessing in the heavenly places in Christ" (Ephesians 1:3). And many-a-time you are blessed by God's good grace to receive that for which you ask!

Beloved, God is at work in you through your trials and disappointments, too. But because He is God, He is able to take what is dark, bitter, and painful and make something beautiful of it. Indeed, that is the Master Weaver's specialty! Count on it...and praise Him for it, too!

Threads of Sacrifice

"I also have lent him to the LORD;
as long as he lives he shall be lent to the LORD."
1 SAMUEL 1:28

O ne of my favorite books is entitled *The Hidden Price of Greatness*.[1] This book details the suffering in the lives of many Christians who are considered today to be heroes of the faith, people like Martin Luther, John Wesley, and Augustine. As I consider the lives of these saints who became martyrs and fugitives because of their faith, it truly seems that joy shines the brightest in the person whose life has been darkest.

And oh, what dark, sad colors have appeared so far in the life-tapestry of Hannah, one who loved God so!

Threads of Joy

We are surprised by a splash of brilliance! At the edge of the blackest black, a new color—the riotous threads of joy—appears. And quite a sizable patch it is!

As you know, despite her deep love for God, Hannah had known dark times. She had problems at home where her husband, Elkanah, divided his love between her and another wife. She had personal problems as, year after year, she bore no children to love. She had people problems as the other wife—who had given Elkanah several sons and daughters—relentlessly mocked and reviled her. And she had problems in public when the temple priest scolded her after she prayed (1 Samuel 1:14).

Joy, however, burst on the scene when Hannah received the priest's blessing and later "conceived and bore a son" (verse 20). Never, never, never would Hannah forget who had given her this precious baby. She had prayed, and God, the Creator of life, had heard her prayers and answered with the gift of her son. So Hannah named him *Samuel*, meaning "name of God" and "asked of God," saying, "Because I have asked for him from the LORD" (verse 20). Samuel would continually remind his devoted and prayerful mother of God's mercy toward those who call upon His name.

Do you share Hannah's joy? Even if the weaving of your life contains many dark threads, can others see the brilliance of joy? Can you thank the Lord for His goodness and mercy? The psalmist calls himself and us to "bless the LORD, O my soul, and forget not all His benefits" (Psalm 103:2).

Even if your life is dark right now, consider the charge that Paul gives us believers on this side of the cross. We are to rejoice in the Lord always (Philippians 4:4)—to rejoice in the forgiveness, redemption, and relationship with God that Christ made possible on the cross through His death for you and me. May the brilliant threads of that joy brighten whatever darkness you now know!

Threads of Love

Rich and warm are the red tones, the violets, and the roses in God's spectrum of colors. And those are the perfect tints for the threads of love woven into the spectacular masterpiece of Hannah's humble life.

A baby was born! And this was no ordinary birth. A baby was born to the long-barren Hannah—and she had work to do, and do quickly!

You see, Hannah only had a few brief years to train her son for God. After all, her Samuel had not only been "asked *of* God" and given *by* God, but he had also been *vowed* to God and so must be *given* to God. Exactly how long did Hannah have to pour her love and God's truth into little Samuel? A brief two or three years—only until he was weaned (1 Samuel 1:23).

Question: How does a mother—in Hannah's time or ours—train a child for God?

Answer: By following God's guidelines for child-raising:

1. *Love the Lord with all your heart* (Deuteronomy 6:5). Training a child for God requires that you, dear mother (or grandmother!), love God supremely. You can only give away what you yourself have.

2. *Teach your child God's Word* (Deuteronomy 6:6-7). God's Word will teach, convict, guide, and train your young one as he or she grows (2 Timothy 3:16).

3. *Teach your child God's ways.* Proverbs 22:6 advises, "Train up a child in the way he should go." A mother is to "educate a child according to his life requirements" and "give instruction to a youth about his way."[2] God's way *is* "the way he should go"!

4. *Remember the Lord at all times* (Deuteronomy 6:7). Your own devotion to God and His Son points your child to eternal life. So, in the moment-by-moment unfolding of everyday life, acknowledge God's lordship and power, His sovereignty and love, His protection and provision. Your children will take note!

5. *Worship the Lord* (Deuteronomy 6:13). The habit of worship in your life will instill a habit of worship in your child's life. Worship the Lord openly and often.

Worship the Lord at home and at your church with His people.

Dear loving mother or grandmother, don't let another minute slip by! Set about *now*—do whatever you can *now*—to train each child your life touches for the God you love.

Threads of Sacrifice

Hannah's love flowed warm and full. How she cherished her little boy, never forgetting for a day that Samuel had been asked of God and given to her by Him!

Hannah also never forgot that Samuel must be handed over to God's high priest to serve the Lord every day of his life. As you know by now, when the childless, heartbroken Hannah had petitioned God for a son, she had also promised to give him back to God for a lifetime of service. At last (and perhaps all too soon!) that day arrived.

As she and her husband approached the house of the Lord with their son and the sacrifice required for the fulfillment of her vow, Hannah knew that today she would give God the most personal and remarkable sacrifice of all, the source of her greatest joy. She was giving God her best, most costly gift—her only child, her son, Samuel. As she explained, "I...have lent him to the Lord" (1 Samuel 1:28).

As you picture this little family walking toward Shiloh, imagine the rich red yarns added into the tapestry of Hannah's noble life to mark her costly offering. Red seems the most suitable color for sacrifice—the deep, costly, rare red of genuine sacrifice.

Now, the question is, What can you give to God that costs? Will it be your...

> ❦ *Children?* God gave His only Son (John 3:16), and Hannah gave hers. Have you given your children to God for Him to use in any way and in any place for His service and His purposes?

🪶 *Obedience?* It was Samuel himself who later said, "Has the LORD as great delight in burnt offerings and sacrifices, as in obeying the voice of the LORD? Behold, to obey is better than sacrifice" (1 Samuel 15:22). To what obedience is God calling you?

🪶 *Time?* Time wasted is a theft from God.[3] As every thread is valuable, so is every moment of time.[4]

🪶 *Money?* As he placed his silver on an altar to the Lord, King David revealed his heart for God: "I...[will not] offer...to the LORD my God...that which costs me nothing" (2 Samuel 24:24). Gifts of love cost.

Dear one, hold all things lightly and nothing tightly when it comes to God...and that "all" includes your best, most costly treasures!

Threads of Glory

What really counts in the Christian life? I know I've thought about this question. Well, in Hannah we have a woman who knew the answer to this question. She shines forth from the pages of Scripture as a woman who knew pain and problems (barrenness, persecution, misunderstanding, loss), yet gave glory to God when she spoke. As our brave Hannah entered her hardest hour—the hour appointed for her to leave her long-awaited and much-prayed-for son at the house of the Lord to be raised by another—we see that her focus was not on herself, not on her problems, and not on her sacrifice, but instead on her great God. Expressions of exultation and glory tumbled out of Hannah's thankful heart as "Hannah prayed." She heralded, "My heart rejoices in the LORD....I rejoice in Your salvation" (1 Samuel 2:1).

Clearly, Hannah's heart was riveted on God, so we shouldn't be surprised by her worship and praise even at this difficult moment. Her lips revealed her heart, and her words are recorded in the pages of God's Holy Scriptures for women through the ages—women just like you and me—to read, to enjoy, to learn from, and to imitate. Note the content of Hannah's impassioned prayer.

> ♪ *God's salvation*—"I rejoice in Your salvation" (verse 1).

> ♪ *God's holiness*—"No one is holy like the LORD" (verse 2).

> ♪ *God's strength*—"There [is no] rock like our God" (verse 2).

> ♪ *God's knowledge*—"The LORD is the God of knowledge" (verse 3).

> ♪ *God's power*—Only God has the power to make the mighty weak, the full hungry, the barren fertile, the dead alive, the sick well, the poor rich, and the humble exalted (verses 4-8).

> ♪ *God's judgment*—"The adversaries of the LORD shall be broken in pieces" (verses 9-10).

What blazing glory you, too, bring to God as you pray and praise as Hannah did! Why not memorize parts of Hannah's psalm of praise and make it your own? Meditate on the attributes and actions of God she mentions there. And make sure that in every event or difficulty you focus on the person and power of God, not on your circumstances. Be confident of God's sovereign and loving control over the events of your life.

Threads of Vision

How does a woman who loves God and her family fill her days when her nest is empty? That's the next challenge Hannah faced. After her many years of suffering, grief, and prayer, God at last graced Hannah with a son. As she loved and trained Samuel, her days were happy, full, and rich. But remember,

Hannah had wanted Samuel so badly that she had vowed to "give him to the LORD all the days of his life" (1 Samuel 1:11). And because her love for God was genuine, Hannah kept that promise and took her young son to the house of the Lord 16 miles away.

Again, how does a woman who loves God and her family fill her days when her nest is empty? Note Hannah's example. Mark it well! Rather than give in to sadness, Hannah worked on long-distance love. Each year she made Samuel a little robe and took it to him (1 Samuel 2:19).

Hannah, whose life was such an exquisite weaving, became a weaver herself—weaving for the next generation. Imagine the rich variety of colors Hannah carefully selected for Samuel's warm and beautiful coats. And imagine the lifetime memories evoked by the necessary darks, the splashes of blue, the sparkling silver and gold, the brilliant yellows, and the crimson reds—memories of the lessons she had learned from the Lord throughout the years. And don't you think Hannah, who prayed so fervently for a son, prayed for him still as she wove his robes? There's no more secure investment in the next generation than your prayers for your children!

Now consider how you can follow Hannah's example. What can *you* do today to love your children and grandchildren across the miles? The mother of writer Elisabeth Elliot prayed and wrote letters. For more than 45 years, she wrote to each of her six children twice a week (that's 12 letters a week—before computers!).[5]

As a loving, praying mother, reach out to your children today—and every day!—with your prayers and your letters and your love. Your faithful efforts are indeed a secure and vital investment in the next generation.

Threads of Growth

Jesus said, "Unless a grain of wheat falls into the ground and dies, it remains alone; but if it dies, it produces much grain" (John 12:24). In Hannah's situation, the "grain of wheat" that fell into the ground and died was her young son, whom she left with the priest at Shiloh (1 Samuel 1:28). Oh, Samuel didn't die in the literal sense, but as we know, Hannah, who was childless for so long, had prayed fervently to God for a son, vowing in the midst of her impassioned prayers to give her baby back to God all the days of his life. Faithful to her word, Hannah did experience, in a sense, the death of her son.

Yet *after* Hannah acted on her vow, *after* she gave her little boy to God, *after* she had apparently lost her only child, "the LORD visited Hannah, so that she conceived and bore three sons and two daughters" (1 Samuel 2:21). Five more children filled Hannah's empty home after Samuel left! The grain of Hannah's sacrifice sprouted and bore fruit—much fruit! Hannah's faith grew, her family grew, her love grew, her joy grew, and her influence grew as she had the opportunity to raise five additional children.

Hannah learned many lessons that are represented by vibrant green threads of growth running throughout the weaving of her life. In this final look at the tapestry of Hannah's life of remarkable sacrifice, allow her to pass on to you several of her lessons in growth for your own tapestry.

～ *Hannah's Message for Your Life Today* ～

1. Hannah learned firsthand the heartache that accompanies barrenness. Are you sympathetic and sensitive to those around you who have no children?

2. Hannah learned to take her problems to God. Do you tell God your problems, or only your friends?

3. Hannah learned about petitioning the Lord. Have you learned the value of earnest prayer and petition (James 5:16)?

4. Hannah learned to pray for God's purposes, and not her own (Matthew 26:42). Have you learned this valuable life lesson yet?

5. Hannah learned that children are gifts from the Lord. How does the fact that your children are gifts to you from God impact your parenting (Psalm 127:3)?

6. Hannah learned the importance of training up a child for God. Are you diligently training your children—on loan to you from God—for service in His kingdom?

Esther

~

Remarkable Courage

The Beauty of Courage

"If I perish, I perish!"
ESTHER 4:16

~

ot only do women love the study of the beautiful
Esther, but so do their daughters, no matter what
their ages. Why? Because Esther, the exquisite Old
Testament queen and heroine, was truly a "star," as her name
indicates. She was beautiful, brave, obedient, respectful, and
wise. And she was the woman God chose to use to help save
His people, the Jews. What does it take to acquire the beauty
of being useful to God? Esther shows us, and she shows us
that our usefulness to God springs from the same foundation.

The Beauty of Usefulness

> *Heritage*—Esther, a Jew from the tribe of Benjamin, was
> taken to Babylon (or Persia) when her people were led
> away captive around 600 B.C.

> *Consider your own heritage.* What life lessons have you
> learned from what your ancestors stood for, fought for,
> believed in, and endured?

Parentage—Both of Esther's parents died while she was young, but a faithful and loving cousin took her in and brought her up as his daughter.

Consider your own parentage. If you, too, have "missing" parents, gratefully acknowledge those whom God has provided in their place to shape your life.

Tutelage—All of us have been taught by many teachers, and Esther is no exception. She learned not only from her cousin Mordecai, but also from Hegai, a heathen eunuch in King Ahasuerus' palace who taught her the ins and outs of pleasing the king.

Consider your own tutelage. Give thanks for the variety of teachers God has sent your way to instruct you and guide you to the present point of being useful to Him.

Advantage—Esther was gifted with physical beauty, Mordecai's wisdom, and Hegai's preferential treatment.

Consider your personal advantages. Identify those conditions, circumstances, and opportunities God sovereignly arranged to make you useful in His kingdom.

Homage—All said and done, Esther's heritage, parentage, tutelage, and advantage added up to homage when she was presented as King Ahasuerus' queen (Esther 2:17).

Consider the homage you will one day enjoy because you are a member of a royal priesthood (1 Peter 2:9), a daughter of the King of the universe!

Dear one, Esther's God is your God too. As the Omnipotent One, He is always at work in every detail of your precious life. Thank Him now for His active, transforming, loving presence in your life.

The Beauty of Courage

I mentioned Esther's outstanding courage. She is the woman who uttered the famous words, "If I perish, I perish!" (Esther 4:16).

What courage! What maturity of faith in the Lord! This beautiful Jewess was married to a temperamental pagan king. When she learned of a plot to kill all Jews, she knew she must go—unsummoned—before her husband and plead for their lives. Her plan put her in danger because no one (not even a wife!) went before the king uninvited without risking death. Yet her courage, rooted in faith, empowered Esther to boldly say, "If I perish, I perish!" Both the urgent need to act on behalf of God's people and her fearless faith in God inspired Esther's heroism. The result? Esther's life was spared—and so were God's people.

Can you put your name alongside the remarkable Esther, who brilliantly displayed the beauty of courage? Do you value the things of God more than the things of this world? Do you embrace the stance of faith that "for to me, to live is Christ, and to die is gain" (Philippians 1:21)? Could you cry out in the face of death, "If I perish, I perish"? Allow the following words to urge you to a life of greater courage.

> Afraid? Of what?
> To feel the spirit's glad release?
> To pass from pain to perfect peace,
> The strife and strain of life to cease?
> Afraid—of that?[1]

The Beauty of Wisdom

A bit of biblical wisdom states, "By long forbearance a ruler is persuaded" (Proverbs 25:15), and God's beautiful Queen Esther offers us an example of this powerful precept put into practice.

Esther was a Jew who learned that Haman, the right-hand man to her husband, King Ahasuerus, had received permission "to destroy, to kill, and to annihilate all the Jews" (Esther 3:13). Esther also knew that only her husband, the ruler, could intervene to save her life and the lives of her people—and that she must persuade him to do so!

What a beautiful picture of grace, wisdom, and patience God paints in Esther's life as she shows us how to effectively persuade other people by following some practical steps of wisdom.

> *Step #1: Stop*—Before trying to rightly handle a wrong situation, Esther paused. She didn't rush headlong into just any course of action.

> *Step #2: Wait*—Time is a precious asset which cannot be bought. Waiting gave Esther time to gather the facts (Esther 4:5).

> *Step #3: Consult*—Waiting also meant important time for Esther to seek counsel from her wise cousin Mordecai (verses 12-14).

> *Step #4: Pray*—Waiting gave Esther time to fast and pray about her task and how she would approach the king (verse 16).

> *Step #5: Decide*—Time, counsel, and prayer moved Esther to choose a plan of action and move forward with the triumphant attitude of "if I perish, I perish!" (verse 16).

> *Step #6: Act*—Before she asked for what she wanted, Esther prepared a special dinner for King Ahasuerus and Haman to test the waters and assess the king's frame of mind (5:4-5).

> *Step #7: Adjust*—Discerning and sensitive to the situation, Esther wisely waited and prepared yet another dinner

before asking her husband to save her people (verse 8). During this second banquet Esther made her request. And the result, by God's grace working through Esther's wisdom? The king acted to protect the Jews!

Esther's path of wisdom can be yours too. Nowhere in the ten chapters of Esther's story will you find anger or agitation, violence or panic, rashness or reaction. Esther knew that out-of-control emotions do not accomplish God's will. Every woman can stop, wait, consult, pray, decide, act, and adjust. Why not follow this path the next time you face a challenge? Relying on God's wisdom enables you and Him together to accomplish His will in His way.

The Beauty of God's Plan

Where has God planted you? What might your fresh new day hold? You may not be waking up to ideal circumstances, and you may not be in a place you would have chosen for yourself. But wherever you are today, whoever fills your life today, and whatever happens to you today, remember that it is God's plan for you in His larger picture and bigger purposes. Esther learned about the beauty of God's plan as her usefulness to Him and His people grew from seeds sown in the soil of sorrow and pain. Just look at the liabilities in this quick biographical sketch of Esther's life.

> *Born:* A stranger in a strange land, born of captives
> *Parents:* Both her mother and father had died
> *Address:* The king's harem; taken there against her will
> *Position:* Queen to an alcoholic and impulsive pagan king

Although these details suggest that she is an unlikely candidate, God used Esther mightily in His plan. In a time of crisis when the Israelite nation was threatened with extermination, Esther realized that she was the only direct link between the king and her people, the Jews. As queen, Esther occupied an important place at court, so she was exactly the person God could use as an instrument for delivering His people. She had truly "come to the kingdom for such a time as this" (Esther 4:14). Therefore, "Esther arose and stood before the king" (8:4).

You, too, can be used by the Lord today by simply being faithful to Him wherever you are *today*, to the people in your path *today*, in your circumstances *today*. Take the hope of these words to heart *today*. Discover the beauty of being part of God's plan by doing the heroic, as defined in this reading.

The Hero

The hero does not set out to be one. She is probably more surprised than others by such recognition. She was there when the crisis occurred...and she responded as she always had in any situation. She was simply doing what had to be done! Faithful where she was in her duty there...she was ready when the crisis arose. Being where she was supposed to be...doing what she was supposed to do...responding as was her custom...to circumstances as they developed...devoted to duty—she did the heroic![2]

The Beauty of Remembering

A good time-management principle advises us to write all special events on a 12-month calendar at the beginning of each new year. This practice ensures that we remember important occasions with each passing year.

More than 2400 years ago, Queen Esther and her cousin Mordecai did something similar when they established a way of remembering how God had once again delivered the Jews from peril. It had been a dark time for God's people. King Ahasuerus had issued an edict giving his subjects permission "to destroy, to kill, and to annihilate all the Jews, both young and old, little children and women…and to plunder their possessions" (Esther 3:13).

Imagine the heartache! The fear! The mourning! The dread! Life was over for God's people! They could do nothing to save themselves. But, trusting in the Lord, Esther found the courage to ask her husband, King Ahasuerus, to give her people two days to defend themselves against the onslaught. He granted her wish, and the Jews overpowered their enemies (Esther 9).

Now imagine the joy! The jubilation! The sweet taste of victory! The relief! Life was *not* over for the Jews! And to celebrate, the Israelites made the day following their triumph a holiday, a day of feasting and gladness, a day of gift-giving. To make sure the Jews then and in generations to come would never, *never* forget how God had turned their sorrow to joy and their mourning to a holiday, Esther and Mordecai instituted the annual observance of the Feast of Purim. "The Jews established…[that] these days should be remembered" (Esther 9:27-28). To this day, 2400 years later, Purim is still celebrated by Jews around the world. Every year faithful Jews remember God's merciful act of salvation.

And you? Do you make every effort to remember the goodness of the Lord to you and to celebrate His work in your life? Remembering Christmas (God's coming in flesh) and Easter (God's atoning work for your sin) is worthy of your efforts and inconveniences. Spiritual birthdays and baptism dates are other opportunities to commemorate God's involvement in your life. As the psalmist reminds us, "Bless the LORD, O my soul, and *forget not all His benefits*…who redeems your life from destruction" (Psalm 103:2,4). Dear one, make every effort to remember His great goodness and love!

∽ *Esther's Message for Your Life Today* ∽

Hasn't it been exciting to get to know the remarkable Esther, "The Queen of Courage"? The Bible tells us about her exquisite physical beauty—that she "was lovely and beautiful" (Esther

2:7). But the primary message you and I receive and want to take away from dear Esther's life is that only the Lord can create the true beauty that comes from within the heart of a woman such as Esther, the kind of woman you and I desire to be. True, we may not be as beautiful as Esther was (few are!), but we can most certainly cultivate the timeless, inner beauty and character she possessed.

- *The beauty of acceptance*—Although Esther's parents had died, we see in her no hint of bitterness or resentment to spoil her beauty. She accepts her circumstances with grace.

- *The beauty of character*—Scholars describe Esther with words such as *faithful, courageous, pious, wise,* and *resolute*—each a reference to inner character.

- *The beauty of spirit*—Clearly Esther possessed the beauty of a gentle and quiet spirit, which we know is very precious in the sight of God (1 Peter 3:4). Esther exhibited a gracious, cautious, patient, and discreet spirit.

Where does such beauty come from? It comes from a heart that adorns itself with a deep trust in God (1 Peter 3:5) and a reverence for the Lord (Proverbs 31:30). It comes from looking to God for sustenance when times and conditions are difficult (Psalm 55:22). It comes from believing God will enable you when your faith is challenged, death is imminent, or relationships are tense (Philippians 4:13). It comes from knowing that God's grace is sufficient for us, whatever life demands of us (2 Corinthians 12:9-10).

So reach, dear one, for this internal and eternal brand of beauty—the beauty that comes from the Lord—which is available to all of God's women. Reach for it as you study the inspired words of your Bible. Reach for it as you pray. Reach out to the Lord so that the beauty of His strength, faith, courage, and wisdom may fill you.

Elizabeth
~
Remarkable Walk

Consecrated to God

*Elizabeth was "righteous before God, walking in all the
commandments and ordinances of the Lord blameless."*
LUKE 1:6

~

*A*h, Elizabeth! And ah, the New Testament! What a
woman to begin it with!

Elizabeth. Obviously I love this name! And I also love the
woman in the Bible named Elizabeth, meaning "consecrated to
God." As we meet Elizabeth now, we learn that she was a
woman blessed by God with a heritage of kinsmen who loved
God. She "was of the daughters of Aaron" (Luke 1:5). Not only
was Elizabeth from the priestly line of Aaron (Exodus 6:23),
but she was married to Zacharias, himself a priest. Don't you
thank the Lord that the ancestors of this dear couple were
faithful to train them in godliness? Training one's children to
love and serve the Lord is a parent's primary responsibility.

To the Glory of God

As we look at the life of Elizabeth, we'll catch a glimpse of
how her family heritage and faithful training in the truths about

God that were passed on to her (perhaps around "the family altar") prepared and equipped her to walk bravely through a difficult and pain-filled life. One thing we learn about spending time with God is that it...

> ...will send you forth to your daily task with cheerful heart, stronger for the work and truer to duty, and determined in whatever is done therein to glorify God.[1]

Exactly what was it that caused Elizabeth's difficult and pain-filled time? Jumping ahead in her life story, we see that Elizabeth passed the age of childbearing...and never had a child. That statement points to decades of marriage under the dark cloud of barrenness in a culture that considered childlessness both a calamity and God's judgment for sin.

How did Elizabeth keep going? Perhaps her faithfulness to a devotional time with her God exposed her to empowering truths about Him—truths which fortified her for the day-in, day-out reality of her childless life. Only the Lord and the knowledge of Him could have given her a cheerful heart, strength for her work, and the determination to glorify God in all she did, including suffering.

Do you have a daily devotional time? If not, begin today. See that you spend time each day being quiet before the Lord, studying His Word, and praying. Worship Him. Look to Him for strength for the day. And if you have children, gather them daily to pray and hear God's sacred Word. This daily practice will help your children stand strong in the Lord and His truth, seeking to glorify God in all they do.

More Than a Conqueror

Consider God's portrait of Elizabeth and Zacharias. These dear people of God were blessed recipients of a godly, priestly heritage, but they were nevertheless ordained to walk down a difficult road. As we learned, they had no children—no little

ones to love, no grandchildren to cherish, no one with whom
to share their heritage of faith, no offspring to carry forth the
family name.

Despite this painful fact in a time when childlessness was
considered a sign of God's judgment for sin, Luke tells us in no
uncertain terms that Elizabeth and Zacharias, instead of sulking
through life or sinking into bitterness, "were both righteous
before God, walking in all the commandments and ordinances
of the Lord blameless" (Luke 1:6). In other words, they main-
tained a remarkable walk. Despite their painstaking trial, they
were...

- *Righteous*—Elizabeth and her husband followed God's
  law in the most technical sense of strict legal observance.

- *Obedient*—Elizabeth walked alongside her husband in
  all the Lord's commandments (moral obedience) and
  ordinances (ceremonial obedience).

- *Blameless*—Elizabeth and Zacharias lived lives that
  were pleasing to God. Outwardly obedient to the Law
  of Moses, they were also inwardly obedient to the Lord.

But still they suffered. Aren't you glad God tells us about
that suffering? Elizabeth shows us the way to love God and
follow hard after Him even when life is difficult. What con-
tributed to her faith and faithfulness? Perhaps—and possibly
and probably—it was a daily devotional time. Such a time...

> ...will make you conscious throughout the day of
> the attending presence of the unseen Divine One,
> who will bring you through more than a con-
> queror.

Throughout the day, moment-by-moment awareness of
God's unfailing presence with you will enable you to bear

every cross and face every crucible as far more than a conqueror!

Dear one, there is no other way to endure difficult times *and* remain righteous, obedient, and blameless but to visit with the Lord and look to the Divine One...daily, diligently, and devoutly. Seek Him now. Experience what it is to be, in Christ, more than a conqueror as you face life's challenges and hardships.

Strength for Today

The childlessness that Elizabeth and her husband knew may not sound too troublesome to us in a time when many couples choose not to have children. But in Elizabeth's day, the Jewish rabbis believed that seven kinds of people were to be excommunicated from God. Their list began with these searing words: "A Jew who has no wife, or a Jew who has a wife and who has no child." Besides being a great stigma in the Jewish culture, having no children was even valid grounds for divorce.

While a husband could divorce a barren wife, there was a weight much heavier than the fear of divorce in the heart of a woman who had no children. You see, every Hebrew woman hoped to bear the long-awaited Messiah. As a faithful, righteous, and obedient Jew, surely Elizabeth had also dreamed of being so privileged. Sadly, however, the flame on Elizabeth's candle of hope died as her childbearing years flickered out. As the Bible explains, "They had no child, because Elizabeth was barren, and they were both well advanced in years" (Luke 1:7).

How does one cope with discouragement, disappointment, adversity, and blighted hopes, dear pilgrim? By spending time with God! Remember, *Elizabeth* means "God is my oath" or "a worshiper of God" or "consecrated to God." Don't you think she looked to Him for strength for each day? And so must you. That devotional time with God...

...will bring you strength to meet the discouragements, the disappointments, the unexpected
adversities, and sometimes the blighted hopes that
may fall to your lot.

A woman who loves God looks not to the day's problems,
but to the remarkable, supernatural power of her God to assist
her with those problems. Only a quiet visit with God gives you
strength for today, strength to face "the discouragements, the
disappointments, the unexpected adversities, and the blighted
hopes" that may sometimes fall to your lot. The light received
from the Lord each new day fuels our love relationship with
Him, keeps the flame of our hope burning, and kindles
strength for one more day, whatever it may hold.

So, dear precious sister, like Elizabeth, cling to God, whatever your circumstances. And cling to His promise—"Be strong
and of good courage; do not be afraid, nor be dismayed, for
the LORD your God is with you wherever [and through whatever!] you go" (Joshua 1:9).

Bright Hope for Tomorrow

And then something happened in Elizabeth's life. It was a
miracle! No, it was many miracles! Read about them yourself.

First miracle—As Elizabeth's husband, Zacharias, performed
his priestly duty at the temple, a glorious messenger of the
Lord suddenly appeared to him. "Your prayer is heard," he
announced, "and your wife Elizabeth will bear you a son." The
good news continued. "And you will have joy and gladness,
and many will rejoice at his birth. For he will be great in the
sight of the Lord, and...he will also go before Him in the spirit
and power of Elijah" (Luke 1:15,17).

Second miracle—Unfortunately, Zacharias questioned the
angel's glad tidings and was struck dumb for his unbelief
(verses 18-20).

Third miracle—Just as the angelic visitor had predicted, Elizabeth did conceive despite her old age! "Now after those days his wife Elizabeth conceived" (verse 24). What bright hope for tomorrow!

How did Elizabeth respond to the miracle of pregnancy? Did she boast? Did she parade around town, spreading the news? Did she raise her hand and "share" at the local prayer-'n'-share group? No, Elizabeth chose to stay out of sight, nestled quietly near the Lord she loved. "She hid herself five months" (verse 24). Why?

- *She was joyful*—A baby was on the way! And this baby would be the forerunner of the Messiah, who was also on the way!

- *She was grateful*—She may have spent a good deal of those many months at home bowed in thanksgiving before the Lord.

- *She was realistic*—The expected child was to play a mighty part in the history of God's people, and the responsibility of training him in godliness demanded serious and prayerful preparation on her part.

Do you go to the Lord with not only your sorrows, but also with your joys, your gratitude, your responsibilities, and your bright hopes for your tomorrows? Do so, because such a time…

> …will sweeten home life and enrich home relationships as nothing else can do.

God will fill you anew with His love and hope, peace and strength, the fruit of His Spirit, when you spend time with Him—and your home life and family relationships will be sweetly blessed.

Remarkable Walk of Faith

It's a fact—He who is mighty performs great things for those who love Him. So testified Mary, the mother of Jesus (Luke 1:49). And the same is true for you. And that same mighty God accomplished great things for the humble Elizabeth, too. Leading off Elizabeth's "Great Things" list was a miraculous pregnancy in her old age. And then the miracle was complete. When "Elizabeth's full time came...she brought forth a son" (verse 57), who would be known as John the Baptist. And how did the people respond? "When her neighbors and relatives heard how the Lord had shown great mercy to her, they rejoiced with her" (verse 58).

It's hard for us to imagine Elizabeth's complete and utter joy at God's goodness to her. She had been so long without a child, and yet—miracle of miracles—God chose her to bear John, the forerunner of the Lord! Her little baby would grow up to be great in the sight of the Lord, to be filled with the Holy Spirit, to turn the hearts of many in Israel to the Lord, and to make ready a people prepared to receive the Messiah (Luke 1:15-17). The blazing light of God's goodness made many decades of darkness fade into a distant memory.

~ *Elizabeth's Message for Your Life Today* ~

It's been so enlightening to look at Elizabeth's life, to contemplate the depth of her devotional life, to accompany her through her dark times, to learn from her humility, to witness her remarkable walk, and to rejoice with her in God's goodness to her. Let's allow her many messages to sink into our hearts through a series of questions.

> ❧ Do you think about the great things God has done for you? Verse 24 tells us that Elizabeth hid herself for five months to contemplate God's goodness in her life.

❧ If you are a mother, do you consider that role to be one of life's greatest blessings? Do your children bring you great joy? When John was born, his mother's heart was filled with overflowing joy. Elizabeth relished the thought of—at long last—being a mother!

❧ Do you rejoice with others over the great things God does in their lives? Elizabeth's neighbors gathered to rejoice with her over her newborn. The Bible teaches that "love does not envy" (1 Corinthians 13:4) and calls us to "rejoice with those who rejoice" (Romans 12:15).

❧ Do you remain faithful to God and choose to trust in His goodness even in the darkness, even when you see no sign of His love? In times like that, we women who love God are to "walk by faith, not by sight" (2 Corinthians 5:7), choosing to trust in God's redemptive goodness and unfailing love as we wait once again to experience it. Elizabeth's was a remarkable walk of faith, trust, humility, and ultimately, joy. And yours, too, can be a remarkable walk when you give glory to God by trusting in Him...no matter what.

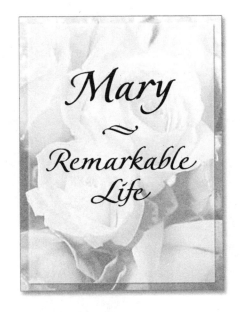

Mary
~
Remarkable Life

Highly Favored One

"You have found favor with God."
LUKE 1:30

~

ruly, no female has ever been as honored around the world as Mary, the remarkable mother of our Lord Jesus Christ. In fact, in 1957, statistics revealed that some 3,720,000 parents had named their daughters Mary or one of its derivatives.[1]

We have much to learn from Mary. We'll be delving into the details of her life a little later, but let's first consider a few facts about this woman. We are initially introduced to Mary, "of whom was born Jesus who is called Christ," when her name appears in "the book of the genealogy of Jesus Christ" and she is referred to as wife to her husband, Joseph (Matthew 1:1,16).

Blessed Among Women

Exactly what kind of woman did God choose to be "blessed...among women" (Luke 1:28), to carry within her womb God-become-man, to love and cherish Him as her first-born son, to raise Him in the knowledge of the Lord God, to be the mother of His precious and only Son?

- *A chaste virgin*—The prophet Isaiah stated that God's Son would be born of a virgin (Isaiah 7:14). Young Mary was unmarried, a pure and godly woman.

- *A humble maiden*—Hailing from the village of Nazareth, Mary was a small-town girl, not a princess from a powerful nation or a sophisticated city girl from the best of society.

- *A devoted follower*—God always looks at the heart, not the outward appearance (1 Samuel 16:7). When He looked at dear Mary, He found in her a woman after His own heart, a woman who would live according to His will (Acts 13:22).

- *A faithful Jew*—Of the tribe of Judah and the line of David, Mary worshiped the one true God and apparently did so in spirit and truth (John 4:24). Only such a woman would qualify for God's important assignment.

As you appreciate and marvel at Mary's life, let yourself enjoy the relief that comes with knowing that, no matter how humble, how simple, how poor, how ordinary, how intelligent, or how successful we are, God looks on our hearts just as He did Mary's. And like her, you can be blessed among women and used by God to do great things for Him. How? Simply love Him...love Him humbly, devotedly, faithfully...love Him with all your heart, soul, strength, and mind (Luke 10:27)!

Priceless Passion

In the previous chapter, we learned that the first people to hear that Messiah, the Savior of the world, was on His way were the faithful elderly couple Zacharias and Elizabeth (Luke

1:17). At long last, 400 years after the last prophecy concerning His arrival, the blessed event was about to happen!

But exactly *how* would He arrive? The answer, in a word, is *Mary*. Little is known about this woman so richly blessed by God to bring His Son into the world. So far we know that the Bible reports that she was a virgin from the city of Nazareth, of the tribe of Judah, of the royal line of David. Let's piece together a few more details of her remarkable life drawn from the culture of Mary's day.

Parents—Although Mary's parents are never mentioned, we can believe, based on Mary's character and knowledge of God's Word, that she came from a godly home of devout Jews.

Training—As they grew up, girls were trained not only in household tasks, but also in the things of the Lord. It is evident in the richness of her praise-filled "Magnificat" (Luke 1:46-55) that Mary knew the Scriptures well and had hidden portions of God's Word in her young heart.

Engagement—Mary was engaged to Joseph in an era when betrothal was binding. The engagement, made official by a signed, written document of marriage, came at least one year before the wedding.

Age—Most Israelite boys married by their late teens, but women wed even earlier. The rabbis, however, had set the minimum age for marriage at 12 for girls.[2] Mary was most likely a young adolescent.

Although she was probably young and, from all appearances, poor, Mary had something priceless on the inside. She was a woman who loved God deeply, obediently, supremely, and passionately. Is it any wonder then, that God chose this woman to bring His Son into the world?

With God, it's always what's inside that counts! When He shines His holy light into the corners of *your* heart, what does He discover there, dear one? Make it your heart's primary desire to nurture a deep, obedient, supreme, passionate love for God! Such love is a priceless and eternal treasure.

Extraordinary Love

Think about it. Think about the kind of woman God chose to be the mother of His only Son. Mary was *young*—unseasoned, inexperienced, unaccomplished, and unmarried. She had never been a mother. Mary was *poor*—possessing no fortune, no wealth, and no family inheritance. Mary was *unknown*—boasting no fame or social status. No one had ever heard of her father or mother—or her. Furthermore, nothing is said about her physical appearance or beauty. Clearly, no one would choose Mary to be the mother of God's Son...except God! Despite what she lacked in the world's eyes, God sent His angel Gabriel to this poor, humble teenage girl (Luke 1:26-27).

Can you imagine the scene? Mary herself could hardly believe her eyes! In fact, the angel Gabriel addressed her amazement, "Do not be afraid, Mary, for you have found favor with God" (verse 30). Imagine what this angelic messenger from God looked like! But more startling was the announcement Mary heard. She could hardly believe her ears either as this magnificent creature uttered, "Rejoice, highly favored one, the Lord is with you; blessed are you among women!" (verse 28).

When the Lord went looking for a woman to bless as mother to His Son, He searched for a woman who loved God. From the world's perspective, Mary seemed completely *un*fit, *un*usable for any task. Do you often feel that way too? You may feel that you are no one special, that you are deficient in areas that the world deems essential, that you need more education, better clothes, a better resumé, a better pedigree—the list goes on. But if you love God—if you seek after Him in your heart—you'll find favor with Him, and He will use you.

Now I ask you, my friend, do *you* want to do extraordinary things for God? Then start by simply loving and obeying Him. Mary's love for God qualified her to be used by God. She was poor, young, and unknown, but she possessed a faith that was pleasing in God's sight, so she found favor with Him. Beloved, when you love God enough to pay the high price of obedience, then you, too, will be highly favored by Him. Just imagine—and pray about—how He might use you!

Turning Points

For Mary, on the remarkable day when the remarkable Gabriel appeared (seemingly out of nowhere!), the sun had risen that morning just as it had risen every day of her life. There she was, possibly considering her list of chores. After all, it was just another routine day. No, there was no hint that on this day her life would be transformed and transported from the mundane and the routine into the realm of the mysterious. But something happened that changed everything forever.

When the angel Gabriel appeared before young Mary, the words he spoke to her completely altered her life. Nothing would ever be the same for Mary, for God had chosen her to be the mother of His Son. She would bring into the world its Savior, Lord, and King. Nothing *could* ever be the same for Mary! No, it was a definite turning point.

All women who love God can learn much from Mary about how to handle the turning points of life. We see in the Gospel of Luke that, at this major juncture in her life, Mary humbly accepted the news from Gabriel that she would bear God's Son. Notice her initial response—"How can this be, since I am a virgin?" (Luke 1:34 NASB). This perfectly natural question received an answer that pointed to the supernatural—"The Holy Spirit will come upon you, and the power of the Highest will overshadow you; therefore, also, that Holy One who is to be born will be called the Son of God" (verse 35). The birth would be a miracle...and that was all the explanation Mary got!

Perhaps you too, dear lover of the Lord, can point to a day in your life that changed everything for you—a day after which nothing was ever the same, perhaps a day when dark clouds hid the sun. There's no doubt that such turning points in life can shake us to the core. But they should also send us to God, His Word, and His promises...and to the acceptance of the fact that full understanding of the "how" and any "whys" lies in the realm of God.[3]

Thankfully, Mary shows us how to accept the unacceptable and how to keep on keeping on after our world seems to come to a screeching halt. Read on.

The Heart of a Handmaiden

Exactly how does one face a challenge? How does one respond to a request from God—a life-changing request? Mary, who faced the incredible challenge of being the mother of Jesus, God's own Son, shows us the way. Remember, after asking her one-and-only, perfectly natural question, she received word that Jesus' birth would be by a mystery and a miracle. What would you do or say next, my friend? Again, Mary shows us how as she humbly accepted the news from God's angel Gabriel. Two clues found in the Scriptures help us understand how Mary was able to put her faith in her God at this life-changing moment.

> *Clue #1: The Heart of a Handmaiden*—After God's messenger told Mary her part in God's glorious plan, her first words were, "Behold the maidservant of the Lord!" (Luke 1:38). In the Bible, *maidservant* or *handmaid* refers to a female slave whose will was not her own. Instead, she was obligated to perform her master's will without question or delay. A handmaiden would sit silently, watching for hand signals from her mistress (Psalm 123:2), which she would obey without question or hesitation.

Clearly, Mary had cultivated the heart of a handmaiden and a devoted attentiveness to her Lord. No longer regarding her will as her own and instead considering herself as having no personal rights, she was wholly committed to her God. Her one purpose in life was to obey her Master's will.

So that day in Nazareth when God moved His hand and signaled His will, His devoted young handmaiden noticed and responded. A model for every woman who loves God, Mary accepted God's will for her life. Whatever God wanted, this humble handmaiden was willing to do, even though obedience meant that everything in her life changed forever.

Spend some time in prayer. Ask God to help you let go of those circumstances of your life that you don't understand... and to embrace His good, acceptable, and perfect will for you (Romans 12:2). Thank Him for what He is teaching you through the life of Mary. Ask Him to continue to teach you to love—and trust—Him even more and to grow in you the heart of a handmaiden.

An Attitude of Acceptance

But there's more to putting your faith in God at a life-changing moment. Beyond developing the mentality of a handmaiden toward God, we must also cultivate another amazing characteristic that we witness in the young Mary.

> *Clue #2: An Attitude of Acceptance*—Having acknowledged herself as "the maidservant of the Lord," Mary then said to God's representative, "Let it be to me according to your word" (Luke 1:38).

When God spoke through Gabriel and told Mary that she had been chosen to be the mother of Jesus, she willingly accepted God's plan for her, and her life was transformed completely. God's choice meant that Mary would be pregnant before she was married; therefore, she would be branded a fornicator (John 8:41). God's choice meant trouble with her husband-to-be, trouble at home, trouble in Nazareth, and trouble among the children she would one day have. His choice meant a life of tension as she and her baby were hunted down, as she fled from country to country, and as her first-born son caused violent reactions in the hearts of the people He met. And God's choice meant that Mary's soul would be pierced with great sorrow (Luke 2:35) as she followed her son on His path of pain to the foot of the cross (John 19:25). Yet when the angel appeared with his news, Mary's attitude of acceptance was clear. "Let it be to me according to your word."

∿ Mary's Message for Your Life Today ∿

Do you wonder why Mary was able to accept God's radical plan for her life? Mary's own words answer that question. She saw herself as God's handmaiden and, as such, accepted His will for her life. Furthermore, Mary knew her heavenly Father well enough to trust Him, to rest in His love for her, and to accept what He ordained for her life. Remarkable!

And you, dear friend? Is yours an attitude of servanthood and acceptance? Prayerfully consider this checklist:

- How do you generally handle shocking news or unfair circumstances?

- What keeps you from replying to the events of life with "let it be to me according to your word"?

- What could you do to learn more about the character of our trustworthy God?

- What step toward that goal will you take today?

O Worship the King!

"My soul magnifies the Lord."
LUKE 1:46

~

*W*henever I teach from Titus 2:3-5, the passage in the Bible that speaks of "the older women" teaching "the young women" in the church, I can't help but point to the sweet sisterhood and tender relationship between the dear Mary, who was oh-so-young, and her cousin Elizabeth, who was oh-so-old. We've already met Elizabeth, so I'm sure you'll agree that both Elizabeth and Mary were women who loved God. And both were pregnant—*miraculously* pregnant—Elizabeth with the one who would announce the coming of Jesus, and Mary with the Lord Himself. What sweet fellowship these two lovers of the Lord enjoyed in Elizabeth's home-sweet-home.

God is truly the Master Weaver, and I invite you to watch as He weaves together the lives of two women who loved Him, two women who worshiped Him. Truly, the women's friendship illustrates God's design that His older women encourage the younger ones in just such a May–December relationship.

May and December

Now, how did Mary come to be in Elizabeth's home-sweet-home? Following the angel Gabriel's announcement concerning the baby Mary would have, he mentioned to her that "Elizabeth your relative has also conceived a son in her old age; and this is now the sixth month for her who was called barren" (Luke 1:36). So, off Mary went to visit Cousin Elizabeth. And then an amazing thing happened as Mary "entered the house of Zacharias and greeted Elizabeth" (Luke 1:40). As she crossed the threshold into Elizabeth's warm and welcoming home, the give-and-take of blessing and encouragement, of assurance and edification, of praying and sharing, of *koinonia* and godly fellowship, began. It's been said that a heart that consistently seeks after God "will exert a helpful, hallowed influence over those who may at any time be guests within your home."[1] Certainly such an influence greeted young Mary. Blessed, indeed, was the hallowed influence of Elizabeth's heart and home on her young guest!

And you, precious sister to this twosome. Do you realize that the moments you spend bent over God's Word and kneeling in devoted prayer are a holy time of preparation not only for yourself, but for ministry to others, for ministry within your home? As has been rightly observed, "The greater the proportion of your day—of your life—spent hidden in quiet, in reflection, in prayer, [in study,] in scheduling, in preparation, the greater will be the effectiveness, the impact, the power, of the part of your life that shows."[2] The effectiveness of your ministry to people will be in direct proportion to the time you spend away from people and with God in a quiet time of preparation.

Are you a "May"—a young woman whose love for God is growing? Ask God to lead you to someone older who can fan the flame of your growing love.

Or are you a "December"—a woman who has loving guidance to offer? Seek out those who need your godly influence in their lives.

The Sanctity of Solitude

As we continue on in the forever-recorded story of Elizabeth's hospitality to her younger cousin Mary, remember that Elizabeth, a woman well past the age of childbearing, is expecting a baby. Remember, too, that rather than shouting her good news from her rooftop, Elizabeth chose instead to hide herself for five months to wonder over this wonder.

What do you, dear reader, think Elizabeth did there, huddled alone at home? Don't you suspect that she lingered in worship before God, joyfully exalting Him who is the Giver of all good gifts and the Source of every blessing? In such secluded moments of adoration, Elizabeth, a woman who loved God, exemplified yet another reason for solitary spiritual preparation at home with the Lord:

> We honor Him who is the giver of all good and
> the source of all blessings.[3]

The lovely Elizabeth sought the Lord in the seclusion of her home, privately praising Him that the Messiah was on the way and thanking Him for her baby who was destined to prepare God's people for the Christ's coming.

It was into such a godly environment that Elizabeth's cousin, the also-expectant Mary, arrived, possibly wondering if the events of the past few days of her young life were real. As Mary entered, "when Elizabeth heard the greeting of Mary… Elizabeth was filled with the Holy Spirit" (Luke 1:41), giving Elizabeth an extraordinary understanding of the situation. She greeted Mary with utmost joy and not a hint of skepticism…or jealousy!…about the working of the Lord. As the babe in her womb leaped for joy in response to the Holy One in Mary's, Elizabeth understood the response of her unborn child and acknowledged the great importance of the Christ Child whom Mary carried. The illuminating work of God's Spirit in Elizabeth's carefully prepared heart led to discernment, insight, and understanding about God's will. Her quiet time alone with her God enabled her to believe in His amazing plan...and to rejoice!

Surely you, too, desire to love God more deeply. Seek the sanctity of solitude and allow God to open your eyes that you may behold wondrous things from His law (Psalm 119:18) and His working in your life and in the lives of others. Such time alone with your heavenly Father does indeed honor Him, the Source of all the blessings you know.

Souls Drawn Upward

Once God's plan was set in motion—a plan involving both Elizabeth and Mary—and once these two remarkable women came together for a visit, joyful sparks began to fly! Their Spirit-filled encounter was electric as they offered up adoration to God from their hearts. Consider the scene...

Both Mary and Elizabeth are filled with the Spirit of God, and each is miraculously expecting a baby whose role is central to God's eternal plan for His people. So it's no surprise that, at this moment, the souls of both are drawn upward in worship of the Almighty. In the shelter of Elizabeth's home and beginning with Elizabeth's words of greeting to Mary, "Blessed are you among women, and blessed is the fruit of your womb!" (Luke 1:42), these two cousins-in-the-flesh and sisters-in-the-Lord communed with their God, drawing much-needed strength from Him as well as from one another. Imagine the elation as they shared in their glorification of the omnipotent God. Consider the rich sisterhood in the Lord they shared and how that was enhanced by God's visible work in their lives. Note too the sweet ministry they offered to one another in the quiet retreat of Elizabeth's home.

Sounds like a lovely moment, a sweet relationship, a tender time, doesn't it? But, dear one, they *needed* it and would possibly remember and cling to it often as darker days arrived. Church history suggests that Elizabeth would soon see the death of her husband, and she would soon follow him, enjoying only a brief taste of motherhood. And Mary's soul would be pierced through with sorrow (Luke 2:35) as her precious Jesus walked the path to Calvary's rugged cross.

Do you have such a Mary or Elizabeth who is a friend in Christ? More importantly, are you such a friend to others? The Christian art of encouragement is both a command to be obeyed and a gift God graciously gives to His people. As we who are God's pilgrims walk through treacherous valleys and clouded byways, we are to strengthen and be strengthened by one another in the Lord.

Heart Song

Once Elizabeth spoke her greeting, it was Mary's turn to worship the Lord. As she arrived at Elizabeth's residence, this young woman—who pondered things in her heart and, in biblical accounts, rarely spoke (Luke 2:19)—opened her mouth and spoke from the abundance of her heart.

And what issued forth? Her rich words of praise in Luke 1:46-55 is a song known as the "Magnificat." "My soul magnifies the Lord," Mary began. And take note—the inspired words that followed contained 15 quotations from the Old Testament. As one author has observed, the number of Scriptures quoted in the "Magnificat" shows that "Mary knew God, through the books of Moses, the Psalms and the writings of the prophets. She had a deep reverence for the Lord God in her heart because she knew what He had done in the history of her people."[4]

Clearly Mary had tuned her heartstrings to the heart and the Word of God! Indeed, her heart was saturated with the Word of God. Knowing God and knowing about His mercy, His provision, and His faithfulness to her ancestors, Mary sang! What was the content of her heart song? It was...

- *A song of joy* characterized by gladness and celebration.

- *A song of substance* drawn from the Scriptures.

- *A song from the past* reflecting Hannah's song (1 Samuel 2).

&- *A song for today* since God is the same yesterday and today.

&- *A song for eternity* because God's Word—where Mary's song is recorded—will stand forever!

Knowing God and recognizing His infinite power enables you to join with Mary in her chorus of praise. Why not make Mary's solo a duet? Spend a golden minute now reading her beautiful and joyful words. Then add your voice to her sweet melody and echo her praise: "My soul magnifies the Lord!" The surest test of a heart is indeed the caliber of its speech—the quality of the words that issue forth from it. As Mary's son Jesus would one day say, "A good man out of the good treasure of his heart brings forth good...for out of the abundance of the heart his mouth speaks" (Luke 6:45).

Hallelujah, What a Savior!

But Mary had only begun! You see, Mary's little baby Jesus was the long-awaited Savior. He would take away the sins of the world—including the sins of Mary, His mother! Therefore, this cascading song of her heart begins, "My spirit has rejoiced in God my Savior" (Luke 1:47). Mary recognized that her only hope for salvation was the divine grace of God revealed in His Son, her Messiah.

Perhaps you are wondering, "Why do I—or anyone!—need a Savior?" Consider all that Jesus the Christ, the Savior God sent, offers you and me. He...

> **S**ubstitutes His sinless life for our sinful one (2 Corinthians 5:21),
>
> **A**ssures us of eternal life (John 10:28-29),
>
> **V**anquishes Satan's hold on our lives (2 Timothy 2:26),
>
> **I**nitiates us into the family of God (Galatians 4:4-6),
>
> **O**verthrows the power of sin (Romans 6:1-10), and
>
> **R**econciles us to a holy God (2 Corinthians 5:19).

Are you saved? Do you enjoy in Jesus Christ all that the word *Savior* represents—the forgiveness of sin, the assurance of heaven, freedom from Satan's power, fellowship with the saints, and a relationship with God through His Son? If not, name Jesus your Savior right now! Pray, "Forgive my sins. Come into my heart, Lord Jesus!" You can begin your walk with the Savior today!

And then, whether you have belonged to the Savior for a minute or a lifetime, pause right now. Pray and thank God for the truths touched upon in the SAVIOR acrostic. Sing and shout, "Hallelujah, what a Savior!"

The Beauty of Worship

Worship, or the act of paying divine honors to a deity, "is as old as humanity. It [is]...a necessity of the human soul as native to it as the consciousness of God itself, which impels it to testify by word and act its love and gratitude to the Author of life and the Giver of all good."[5]

And worshiping was exactly what Mary, the mother of our Savior, was doing those 20 centuries ago when she spoke her famous "Magnificat." Her full heart continued offering words of love and gratitude to the Author of life and Giver of all good things for the great works He had done and now was doing for His people and for her.

Do you ever wonder how to express your appreciation to your Savior? He has done so much for us, His beloved children. We were lost, and He found us. We were spiritually blind, but now we see. We were dead in our trespasses and sins, and He has made us alive (Ephesians 2:1). He has called us out of darkness into His marvelous light (1 Peter 2:9). And He has given us sufficiency in all things (2 Corinthians 9:8), blessed us with all spiritual blessings (Ephesians 1:3), and opened the door to abundant life in Him (John 10:10).

So why not do as Mary did and fall before Him now in praise and worship? Remember and name specifically the many awesome things God has done for you, dear woman who loves Him and is loved by Him.

Also think about what acts of worship you can offer Him today and every day—acts that befit such a mighty, protecting, saving, and loving Lord. Consider these possible gifts of worship:

> *Time*—in His Word, in service, in prayer.

> *Money*—given not for a tax deduction or a cause or a person…or for attention, but given solely out of love for God.

> *Faith*—for the future, to offer a sacrifice, or to give extravagantly.

> *Witnessing*—to those who know Him not.

> *Praise*—to Him for all to hear, praise for what He has done for you.

O worship the King now! Extravagantly! Loudly! Sincerely! For, in the words of Mary, "He who is mighty has done great things" for *you* (Luke 1:49)!

～ Mary's Message for Your Life Today ～

It's obvious, isn't it, that Mary knew God, loved God, followed God, and worshiped God. Truly her Magnificat was a hymn of faith. As her mind, heart, and mouth continued its outpouring of pure worship at the thought of Jesus Christ, the Messiah, her little baby-to-be, dear Mary went on to list many of God's attributes, continuing to send us messages of faith and about faithful worship.

> ❧ *God's holiness*—"Holy is His name!" (Luke 1:49)—God is wholly pure and totally "other," set apart from sinful, self-centered human beings. In Jesus, God revealed His holiness.

❧ *God's mercy*—"His mercy is on those who fear Him from generation to generation" (verse 50)—Behold the patience and the mercy of the Lord! In Jesus, God extended His mercy to us in the act of salvation, His Son's death on the cross for our sin.

❧ *God's power*—"He has shown strength with His arm; He has scattered the proud in the imagination of their hearts. He has put down the mighty from their thrones, and exalted the lowly" (verses 51-52)—Stand in awe of God's power! In Jesus, the proud and mighty are put down, while those who in the world's eyes are of low degree, the poor and the humble, are exalted.

❧ *God's goodness*—"He has filled the hungry with good things, and the rich He has sent away empty" (verse 53)—God is good, and Jesus' life and teachings reflect that goodness. He taught that God is kind even to the unthankful and evil (Luke 6:35).

❧ *God's faithfulness*—"He has helped His servant Israel, in remembrance of His mercy, as He spoke to our fathers, to Abraham and to his seed forever" (verses 54-55)—God is eternally faithful to His Word and to His chosen people. In Jesus, God sent the Redeemer He had promised to Abraham and to us, Abraham's seed.

Dear sister, worship the King yourself, as did Mary in her remarkable Magnificat! And get to know these things about God—and more!—by personally studying His Word, the foundation for faith.

A Woman After God's Own Heart

"And she brought forth her firstborn Son."
LUKE 2:7

≈

And she brought forth her firstborn Son, and wrapped Him in swaddling cloths, and laid Him in a manger" (Luke 2:7). These much-loved words, breathed by God, speak of an event that changed the course of history, the fate of man, and the path of our lives. Yet the path Mary walked to the manger was not an easy one.

The Path of Faith

The most wonderful thing that could happen to a young woman happened to Mary. She was chosen by God to bring Jesus, His only Son and His best gift to mankind, into the world! But consider what Mary encountered on that road to the stable.

- Her husband-to-be wanted to quietly divorce her.

- The timing of the Roman tax caused Mary to make a treacherous trip in her final weeks of pregnancy.

    ❧ Mary was away from her home—and her family and friends—when it was time to deliver her first child.

    ❧ And because there was no room in the town's inn, the bed for Mary's little baby was an animal stall, a manger!

These are hardly the ideal circumstances for childbirth! But Mary's God transformed each one of these potential stumbling blocks into stepping-stones for her. How?

    ❧ Obeying God, Joseph did not divorce Mary, but stayed by her side.

    ❧ The timing of the tax meant that Mary was in exactly the right place. The prophecy that Immanuel would be born in Bethlehem was fulfilled (Micah 5:2).

    ❧ Mary's family and friends were far away, but her God (and yours) is all-sufficient in all things. He always provides all that we need. He more than adequately stands in as Head of the family of God and is a Friend who sticks closer than any brother or sister, parent or friend.

    ❧ When the world closes its doors to us, God is our refuge (Psalm 46:1), and He provides us with His power whenever we are weak or in need (2 Corinthians 12:9-10).

What difficulties, what potential stumbling blocks, line the path of your life? Oh, please remember to turn to God and lean on Him! Just as He took care of Mary, your faithful, loving, caring heavenly Father will take care of you as you walk your path of faith!

True Treasure

"Good news! Christ the Savior is born!" God wanted this message spread, and He chose a divine means to proclaim the news and an unlikely group to receive it and share it.

On the night of Jesus' birth, God's angels appeared to a group of lowly shepherds. The radiant messengers lighted up the sky with their presence and praise as they heralded the birth of Christ the Lord. Then, wasting no time, the shepherds went to Bethlehem to verify the angels' message. Once they had done so, they broadcast the glad tidings for all to hear. Some who heard the Word of God from the shepherds merely wondered about it, but Mary, Jesus' mother, "kept all these things and pondered them in her heart" (Luke 2:19). She quietly treasured it in her heart.

Do you know what it means to *treasure* something in your heart? It means to guard that thing so surely and steadfastly that, as a result, you will keep it safely and securely. Mary kept the treasure of God's truth so closely and faithfully that it became hers, safe within her heart.

And as she treasured the truth, she *pondered* it. Again and again Mary thought through the words and events, considering how they fit together, comparing them to prophecy, weighing them against what she knew of her God, carrying their messages in her heart.

We noted earlier that Mary appears to have been a woman of few words. Here we see her as a woman who kept the many wonders she saw and heard within her heart, cherishing them because they came from God. As you read about the birth of Jesus in Luke 2, an account probably told to the Gospel writer by Mary herself, aren't you glad that she treasured and pondered the events surrounding the birth of her son, your Savior? That act of treasuring gave us details about our Savior that now we, too, can hold dear to our hearts!

> Prayer—*O Lord, may Mary's valuable habit of treasuring and pondering Your truth become mine! May I be a woman who loves You and loves Your Word. May I use the mind You've given me to think on what is true, to hide that truth in my heart, and to seek to better understand it.*

A Woman After God's Heart

God never makes a mistake, and He certainly didn't make one when He chose Mary to be the mother of His Son!

The responsibility of raising Jesus, the Righteous Branch of David, called for righteous parents who followed God's law. And that's exactly what Mary and Joseph did. The Bible reports "they brought Him to Jerusalem to present Him to the Lord...and to offer a sacrifice according to...the law" (Luke 2:22,24). As these and other verses in Luke reveal, Mary and Joseph clearly fulfilled the temple rituals required by the law of the Lord following Jesus' birth.

- Jesus was circumcised exactly eight days after His birth, just as God's law required.

- Mary's purification after childbirth took place exactly 40 days after the birth of her male child, and the prescribed sacrificial offering (a pair of turtledoves) was made, just as God's law required.

- Mary presented Jesus, her firstborn son, to the Lord exactly according to the requirements of God's law.

In Mary we see the kind of woman God delights in—a woman after His own heart, a woman willing to do all His will (Acts 13:22). While it's true that, because of Jesus Christ's perfect fulfillment of God's law, we live in the age of God's marvelous grace, our obedience and wholehearted commitment to walking in the ways of the Lord are still essential. Are you one who loves God by walking in His ways? For instance, Do you love others? All of God's law is fulfilled in one word—*love* (Galatians 5:14)!

Do you confess sin instantly, consistently, and sincerely? Fellowship with God is all the sweeter when we confess our sin immediately and then turn completely away from it (1 John 1:9).

Are you faithfully training your children in the nurture and admonition of the Lord? God's primary command to parents is to teach and train our children in His truth and His ways (Ephesians 6:4). Spend time with the Lord now and affirm your desire to be, like Mary, a woman after God's own heart.

The Price of God's Favor

None of us knows exactly what the future holds, but God allowed Mary a hint about what awaited her—a sword would pierce her soul. True, Mary was highly favored by God and greatly blessed to be the mother of His Son, but this privilege also meant real agony. Her joy would be mingled with sorrow.

It was a day of great bliss when Mary and Joseph took their infant son to the temple to dedicate Him to God (Luke 2:22). Surely their hopes and dreams soared as they considered His bright future! As if to affirm their thoughts, an old man named Simeon—a devout man of God who worshiped regularly in the temple and waited expectantly to see the coming of the Lord—took Jesus in his arms and prophesied concerning Jesus' ministry to the world.

But as Simeon finished his blessing, he turned to Mary and said, "A sword will pierce through your own soul also" (Luke 2:35). Mary, a woman after God's own heart, would find her heart pierced to its core by what would happen to her son.

We will never fully know the depth or degree of Mary's anguish, but Simeon's choice of words paints a gruesome picture. The word he used for *sword* was the same word found in the Old Testament to describe the giant Goliath's large, broad sword (1 Samuel 17:51). The pain Mary would know when her son was nailed to the cross would be like the pain inflicted by a huge and cruel weapon.

Dear one, here's a sobering lesson for us—God's blessings on another woman are never cause for jealousy or envy. A woman who is blessed by God, who shines for Him and radiates His favor, may tempt us in our sinfulness to respond with scorn, disdain, or pettiness. But be assured that God's great blessings tend to come at great prices. Perhaps that is why the

Bible encourages us to highly regard those we may be tempted to envy and to instead...

- ♪ rejoice with those who rejoice (Romans 12:15).

- ♪ esteem highly those who are over you in the Lord (1 Thessalonians 5:12-13).

- ♪ remember to pray for and be sure to obey those who rule over you (Hebrews 13:7,17).

Beloved, we don't always know the price of God's favor!

Flight by Faith

And Mary's sorrow began sooner than she may have thought! King Herod was angry, *exceedingly* angry. He was so angry when he learned of a child being called "King of the Jews" that he ordered the murder of every male child under the age of two in and around the city of Bethlehem (Matthew 2:16). Surely the threat of another king would be eliminated by such a command!

But in a dream, God had already instructed Joseph—the sacred infant's earthly guardian—to take his family and flee immediately to Egypt. There they would escape Herod's deadly plan. And Joseph acted! He "took the young Child and His mother by night and departed for Egypt" (Matthew 2:14).

We never know what marriage, motherhood, or even a given day will bring, do we? Mary—a woman who loved God, who was "highly favored" and blessed among women, who had "found favor with God," a woman after God's own heart—nevertheless had lessons to learn about faith in God and following Him.

First, following—Can you imagine being awakened in the middle of a dark night by your husband's declaration that you were leaving, moving—*right now?*

"But where are we going, Honey?"

"To Egypt. It's *only* a 10- to 15-day journey."

"But why, Honey?"

"Because, you see, I had this dream, and God told me to go."

Imagine what would happen under most roofs after that kind of announcement and explanation! (What would you have done in those circumstances?) Mary, however, followed God's plan for her as a wife and followed her husband—an act that saved their young son's life.

Next, faith—Do you realize that faith in God is what enables you and me as women who love God to follow our husbands? Just like the holy women of old—women like Mary—who loved God and trusted in Him, we are to adorn ourselves with God's beautiful, submissive spirit and follow our husbands (1 Peter 3:4-6). Faith in God enables us to do so.

> Prayer—*Father, grant that I may be a woman with faith in You that is strong enough to enable me to follow others as they lead me into Your good and acceptable and perfect will. Thank You for working in my life through the leadership of others.*

Joys and Sorrows

The Gospel writer Matthew is the only one to record Mary, Joseph, and Jesus' flight *to* Egypt, and he is understandably the only one who reports their return *from* Egypt to set up their home in Nazareth. Both journeys were prompted in the same divine way. Once again an angel of the Lord visited Joseph in a dream, this time announcing Herod's death and instructing Joseph to take his little family back to the land of Israel.

So back to the Holy Land they went. Joseph "took the young Child and His mother, and came into the land of Israel" (Matthew 2:21), where they settled down in Nazareth, the hometown of both Mary and Joseph. They were home!

Looking back over the past few years, they could thank God for how He had guided them and protected them. But what about the future? Mary indeed would face many of life's joys...and sorrows. It has been well stated, "Motherhood is a painful privilege."[1] Mary would taste

The Joys of...	*The Sorrows of...*
Loving a child	Watching that child die
Raising a child	Not understanding him
Knowing God through Jesus	Witnessing his death for her sins

Oh, there were other joys for Mary—the happy sounds of a brood of children, joyous pilgrimages together to worship the true God, family meals and cozy times gathered around a warm fire, hearing her son—the Son of God—preach, observing His miracles, and later witnessing His resurrection from the dead. But there were other sorrows as well—the death of her husband Joseph; her fellow townspeople's rejection of her son; and letting go of her son to go about His heavenly Father's business.

∽ Mary's Message for Your Life Today ∽

Now the question for you and me is this: How can a woman after God's own heart manage the grief and tribulation life includes? Thank the Lord we have an answer in Mary's messages to our sore hearts! Are you ready?

Through it all, the lows and the highs, the pains and the pleasures, the sorrows and the joys, Mary loved God and looked to Him for His strength that is always made perfect in weakness (2 Corinthians 12:9). Truly, Mary shows us how to trust the Lord as we too walk the unpredictable road of life— a road of joys and sorrows that God uses to conform us into the lovely image of His Son. Take these lessons to heart:

❧ Hide—and treasure—God's Word in your heart.

❧ Obey God's Word.

❧ Submit to God's good and acceptable and perfect will for your life.

❧ Follow those whom God has appointed to lead you.

❧ Nurture a heart of faith.

❧ Trust God's plan...and His timing!

A Portrait of Devotion

*"These all continued with one accord in prayer
and supplication, with the women and Mary
the mother of Jesus, and with His brothers."*
ACTS 1:14

~

Hasn't it been inspiring to see how faithfully and devotedly Mary and Joseph followed God's law? We can learn much from their lives—lessons we can apply in our own hearts and homes!

Let's now fast-forward 12 years and find further evidence of Mary and Joseph's obedience to God and to the law of the Lord, particularly in the area of worship. We see that Jesus' "parents went to Jerusalem every year at the Feast of the Passover" (Luke 2:41).

Sacred Devotion

When Jesus was 12, He joined His parents in worshiping the Lord at Passover. You see, a Jewish boy became a man at age 12, and God required every adult male to attend the annual Passover celebration. Therefore, Jesus went with His faithful-to-the-Law parents. Many wonderful things happened there on the Temple

Mount, but right now let's consider ways we can ensure that ours—like Mary's—is a family that worships together.

Worship—God calls believers to come together on the first day of the week for worship, and He tells us to be careful not to forsake such assembling together (Acts 20:7; Hebrews 10:25). So a wise and godly woman and mother will do whatever must be done to ensure that she and her family worship together regularly. She does exactly what Mary did—she takes her young ones to church!

Observe—God has given the church the foundational rites of baptism and communion (Matthew 28:19; 1 Corinthians 11:23-25). Just as Jesus' parents made sure He observed the Jewish rites and feasts according to God's instructions, we must—for ourselves and for our children—follow the Lord's instructions to us for worship, baptism, and communion.

Celebrate—Does your church mark special seasons of worship like Advent and Lent? Does it celebrate the church anniversary and ministry dedications, revival meetings, praise and prayer meetings, baby dedications or baptisms, worship services on Thanksgiving Eve, Christmas Eve, Good Friday, and Easter morning? Whatever your church chooses to celebrate, be there! These special times of worship will further your family's dedication to God and His church (and your dedication to your local church) as they sow seeds in the soil of sacred devotion.

Every godly mother you meet will tell you that she wishes she had done more during her children's formative years to impress upon their moldable hearts the importance and joy of family life in the church. Begin today…and whatever happens, persevere!

"Mary, Did You Know?"

Jesus' journey to Jerusalem and the time He spent there celebrating Passover is described in nine verses in Luke 2. Those verses hardly begin to describe all the emotion and insight that resulted from that trip. So much happened!

First, imagine the worship. We can be sure it was glorious and meaningful, especially since it was the first time Jesus could participate!

Then, Jesus was missing from the great company of people traveling home to Nazareth together. Only late in the evening of their first day's journey did Mary and Joseph realize that Jesus was not with either parent or with any family member or friend (verse 44). We shudder to imagine the fear and even terror Mary must have felt in her heart! Her young son was alone in that crowded, bustling city!

Next, Mary and Joseph hurried back to Jerusalem, looking for Jesus all along the way. Once in the city, Mary and Joseph spent three frantic days searching for their son (verses 45-46).

At last, they found Jesus in the temple, sitting among the teachers there and calmly interacting with them. And "when they saw Him, they were amazed" (Luke 2:48). Why? Because Jesus, their 12-year-old son, was sitting in the midst of the teachers of His day, interacting with them, even giving them answers (verse 47)!

Then, as any other mother would have, Mary exclaimed, "Son, why have You done this to us? Look, Your father and I have sought You anxiously" (verse 48).

Finally, giving Mary a few more thoughts to ponder in her heart, Jesus spoke the first of His words that are preserved for us—"Why is it that you sought Me? Did you not know that I must be about My Father's business?" (verse 49).

The result? Mary was amazed—literally "driven out of her senses"—and did not understand (verse 50).

Why didn't Mary know? Didn't she remember what the angel Gabriel had said about Him? Didn't she remember what Elizabeth had said about her unborn child? Didn't she remember what the shepherds had told her, what Simeon had prophesied? Didn't she *yet* know?

And you, my friend? Do you know Jesus as not merely a baby in a manger, a wise teacher, or a good man, but as God in flesh, the Savior of the world? O, believe it now!

A High Calling

Even though the young Jesus obviously felt "at home" in His Father's house, and even though He was gaining a more complete understanding of His calling and purpose as the Son of God, the Holy Child still needed a mother and a home. As someone has marveled, "Not even to the angels fell such an honor as to the parents of Jesus!"[1] Instead, the high calling of mothering the Master fell to sweet Mary.

So after leaving the religious teachers there in the temple area, Jesus returned to Nazareth with Mary and Joseph. The Scriptures say, "He went down with them...and was subject to them" (Luke 2:51). That means He was obedient to His earthly mother and father while He lived under their authority. So Mary continued raising Jesus, the Son of God. What exactly did Mary give to the Messiah?

Mary gave Jesus life, humanly speaking. Hers was the body that brought God's precious Son into this world.

Mary gave Jesus a home. The Man of Sorrows—who all too soon would have no place to lay His head, who would make the Mount of Olives His "home away from heaven," and who would (as we'll soon see) spend time at Mary and Martha's house—received from the heart and hands of dear Mary the gift of a home.

Mary gave Jesus a model of godliness. God had carefully selected Mary for the special job of mothering the Master. Surely she who found such favor with the Almighty would model godly virtues in her home and guide those in her care toward a life devoted to Him.

Like Mary, we who have children can give them these same three gifts. Blessed are the offspring raised in such a heaven on earth! Even those of us who have no children can both model godly character and, as the sisters Mary and Martha did for our Lord, give the gift of home to all who enter our doors. Like Mary, the mother of Jesus, we have the high calling to give life, a home, and training in godliness as we serve God and His people.

Devoted to the End

"Yes, a sword will pierce through your own soul also." My, how these words must have suddenly rung loudly in Mary's ears! As you remember, when Mary took the newborn Jesus to the temple in Jerusalem, the elderly Simeon had solemnly pronounced these prophetic words (Luke 2:35). What a wonderful day that had been! Mary and Joseph were so pleased with their tiny baby, so humbled that God had chosen them to care for His Son, and so excited to present Jesus to God. Simeon himself was ecstatic in the blessing of being able to see the long-awaited Messiah. Yet there had been that word, spoken directly to Mary, about a piercing sword. And now, 33 years later, she felt their full agony!

Yes, Mary's path as the mother of Jesus had many precious moments and held many sacred memories. But that path had its pain, too, as she witnessed people's violent reactions to Jesus and His message. And in the fulness of time—God's preordained, appointed time—Mary found herself standing at the foot of Jesus' cross, watching her firstborn son die a criminal's torturous death (John 19:25). A sword was indeed piercing her soul!

Then, in the horrible quiet, Mary heard the clear voice of Jesus speaking to His disciple John. And He was speaking about *her:* "Behold your mother!" (verse 27). No, she (by now a widow) wasn't being forgotten or overlooked! God was taking care of her! Having loved His own, Jesus loved them to the end (John 13:1), and "His own" included His mother, Mary!

Dear one, consider two lessons from Mary's difficult life that we can take with us along life's often painful path.

Lesson #1—Life's pain should never allow us to neglect caring for our loved ones. Jesus shows us that. Despite the agonizing pain He felt as He hung dying on the cross, He was thinking of Mary, and He called John to provide for her.

Lesson #2—Life's pain should never cause us to doubt God's care for us. The Almighty is with us always, even to the end of the age (Matthew 28:20), and He will not fail to provide for us (Psalm 23:1) or to love us to the end.

Thank God for His unfailing love and care for you...and then follow His example by caring for your loved ones, even in the midst of your own personal pain.

A Portrait of Devotion

Partings are indeed such sweet sorrow, aren't they? And here we are, saying farewell to Mary, the mother of Jesus. She isn't mentioned again in the Bible after this Scripture passage in Acts 1:14—"These all continued with one accord in prayer and supplication, with the women and Mary the mother of Jesus, and with His brothers." Let's examine carefully the details of her final appearance.

Fact #1—Mary is in the upper room. Perhaps the very spot where Jesus shared His last meal with His disciples, this room became the meeting place for His followers after His glorious resurrection.

Fact #2—Mary is among Jesus' faithful followers. No single believer in Christ is ever more important than another. Here we see Mary and others who followed Jesus standing on equal ground.

Fact #3—Mary is praying. Kneeling shoulder-to-shoulder with the other saints, Mary joins with the group, persisting in prayer for much-needed strength and the grace to carry on without Jesus.

Fact #4—Mary is with other women. Jesus' followers included a small band of women who supported His ministry, as well as the wives of some of the disciples.

Fact #5—Mary's other sons are present. We can imagine Mary's joy! Her sons had never believed in Jesus before His death (John 7:5), but they were brought to faith by His death and resurrection. Finally all her sons were united in faith!

What a beautiful—and remarkable!—portrait of godly devotion we find in the life of Jesus' beloved mother. Mary worshiped and fellowshipped with other believers, persisted in prayer, spent time with sisters in the faith, and valued her family's faith. Do these phrases describe your life too? If not, which areas do you need to develop so that your life reflects your devotion to God just as precious Mary's did?

(P.S. Aren't you glad that we never have to truly say goodbye to the remarkable women in the Bible who loved God, women like dear Mary? They are preserved forever in God's Word, and we can renew our acquaintance with them any time by simply opening up our Bibles. Why not make it your practice to take time each day to drop in on one of these women who loved God? Why not refresh your memory of their messages to your life today?)

∽ *Mary's Message for Your Life Today* ∽

How does one wrap her arms around the bigger-than-life, yet oh-so-humble life of Mary? As I thought and prayed about "wrapping up" Mary's remarkable life, I decided to review the few pieces and segments that we've covered together in this book. I want us to take Mary's messages with us along the path He asks us to travel.

Highly Favored One—Why was Mary addressed as "highly favored one" by the angel Gabriel? And why did Mary find "favor with God"? Because she was humble, submissive to God's will, and possessed the heart of a handmaiden. Truly, the way up is down!

O Worship the King—Never forget that Mary's was a soul drawn upward! She loved God's Word, faithfully hid it away in her heart as precious treasure, verbalized it as she magnified the Lord, and exuberantly worshiped the God of her salvation.

A Woman After God's Own Heart—Only the obedient heart is a heart after God! And dear Mary obeyed God and His Word and His leading at every possible opportunity (and in every possible trial!). Mary proved to be a woman after God's own heart as she faithfully followed the path God asked her to walk.

A Portrait of Devotion—No one would ever deny that Mary was, by God's grace, dedicated and devoted to God, to the keeping of His law, to her family, to Jesus, her son and her Savior, and to prayer as a member of the newly formed church, the body of Christ.

Dear friend, if we could only take away these few life-lessons from Mary, you and I—and those around us—would never be the same! So I ask you to "bind them around your neck" and "write them on the tablet of your heart" (Proverbs 3:3). Let's change the world! Let's turn it upside down! Let's live a remarkable life of faith…to the glory of God!

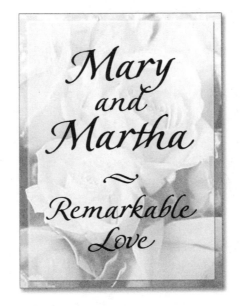

Mary and Martha

~

Remarkable Love

Two Faces of Love

"And [Martha] had a sister called Mary."
LUKE 10:39

～

Our world today offers women—even women who love God—pressure from many sources. We never seem to have enough time—pressure! We want to do well as a wife and a parent—pressure! We are called to be good stewards of finances and effective managers of a home—pressure! How do *you* handle the pressures of life—with peace or panic?

Peace or Panic?

In sisters Mary and Martha, God presents us with a classic study in opposites when it comes to managing the demands of life. Their story begins with these words: "A certain woman named Martha welcomed [Jesus] into her house. And she had a sister called Mary" (Luke 10:38-39). Then what happened? When Jesus went to their home, Martha welcomed Him in for dinner, but she became distracted by all her preparations. Busy in the kitchen, dealing with the multitude of details on her mind, and anxious that everything go well, Martha was a whirlwind of activity.

245

How did her lack of peace show itself? First of all, Martha was stirring the pot not only in the kitchen, but also in the family room! There she stood, accusing Christ ("Do you not care...?"—verse 40) and accusing Mary ("My sister has left me to serve alone"—verse 40), complaining about the burden she had assumed. She's bossy, blaming, distracted from what mattered most. And she's yarping—which, you'll notice, is "pray"ing spelled backward!

In contrast to this hurricane of female hyperactivity, we find the lovely Mary...

— resting at the Lord's feet while Martha is restless.

— worshiping while Martha worries.

— at peace while Martha's panic level rises.

— sitting while Martha is stewing.

— listening while Martha is lashing out.

— commended by Jesus while Martha is confronted by Him (verses 39,41).

Which would an outside observer see in you as you cope with life's schedules, commitments, and pressure? Martha or Mary? Are you normally in turmoil—or are you trusting and at peace? Are you prone to running around in circles—or do you rest in the Lord? Is your relationship with Jesus your first priority—or are you too busy to sit at His feet and enjoy His presence? The woman whose heart and soul are at rest is the woman who knows one theological truth: *Her times are in God's hands* (Psalm 31:15). And this truth makes all the difference when it comes to peace or panic![1]

The Ultimate Resource

Let's move on in evaluating the way we handle the trials of life. What do you do when trouble comes your way? How do you handle the problems that touch your life? For instance, do you tend to...

> ...tell a friend?
> ...call a counselor?
> ...join a group?
> ...go shopping?
> ...get a new hairstyle?
> ...take a pill?
> ...hide in a novel?
> ...watch a movie?
> ...fall apart?
> ...eat something?

The two sisters, Mary and Martha, faced real life-and-death trouble. We've already witnessed Mary and Martha's hospitality as they welcomed Jesus and His disciples into their home for a meal. True, that wonderful day almost turned into a crisis, but they had to face a much worse crisis as a family. You see, their beloved brother, Lazarus, became sick (John 11:1). Besides being dear to them, he was probably their sole means of support. (The Bible never mentions that Mary or Martha has a husband or children.) Their brother's serious illness meant not only great sadness, but an unknown, insecure future as well.

What to do? These two remarkable sisters knew they must tell Jesus. They knew of His deep love for their brother (verse 5), and they knew of His powerful miracles. So they sent for the Teacher.

O that we would follow in this wise pair's footsteps! Why should we turn solely to a friend, a counselor, or a support group when we have Jesus, the Friend who sticks closer than a brother (Proverbs 18:24)? Why should we women who profess to love and trust God dabble in the world's quick fixes and appealing escapes (pleasure, entertainment, vanity) when we face serious trouble? And why should we give in to the flesh when we have the Ultimate Resource in God? As a simple message from an eloquent psalm reminds us,

> I will lift up my eyes to the hills—
> From whence comes my help?
> My help comes from the LORD,
> Who made heaven and earth.
> (Psalm 121:1-2)

May the psalmist's pattern be ours as we follow the example of Mary and Martha and call on Jesus, the Ultimate Resource and Friend, when problems arise and crises come.

A Lesson in Faith

What do you think of when you hear the phrase "the odd couple"? This phrase has come to describe two people who handle life in contrasting ways. Well, my friend, sisters Mary and Martha certainly qualify as an "odd couple." Take, for instance, the scene when Jesus and His disciples visited their home for dinner. We saw Martha bustling with unbridled energy, while Mary instead delighted in worshiping at the feet of the Master.

And now we catch this "odd couple" in another life situation as their brother Lazarus lay seriously ill. Mary and Martha had sent for Jesus, but He did not come. The result? Their beloved brother died. At that point the sisters heard that Jesus was approaching their village. Let's look first at Martha's response and then consider Mary's.

How did Martha respond—or, perhaps in her case, how did she *react*—when she learned that the Savior was approaching? "Martha, as soon as she heard that Jesus was coming, went and met Him" (John 11:20). True to form, Martha *leaped* up, *rushed* out the door, and *ran* down the road to meet the Master!

Martha's statement of faith—Martha may have been abrupt and hurried, but her heart was right. She believed in Jesus and trusted in His power to heal. "Lord," she ventured, "if You had been here, my brother would not have died" (verse 21).

Martha's lesson in faith—Martha was right to go to Jesus, but she had missed a central truth about Jesus. When she volunteered, "I know that whatever You ask of God, God will give You" (verse 22), Jesus corrected her by stating, "I am the resurrection and the life. He who believes in Me, though he may die, he shall live" (verse 25). He was saying, "Martha, I don't have to ask of God. *I am God,* and life is in *Me!* He who believes in *Me* shall live!"

Precious one, who do you believe Jesus is? Martha recognized His power, but her understanding of His deity was incomplete until He corrected her. Do you believe that Jesus is God—God-in-flesh—and that belief in Him, though you die, gives you eternal life? That is the message dear Martha heard from the lips of the incarnate God Himself, and it is His message to us too. As Jesus asked Martha (verse 26), "Do you believe this?"

Fruit Grown in the Shade

We now know how Martha, one member of the "odd couple" of sisters, responded to Jesus after her brother's death. Almost on cue, the energetic, do-it-yourself Martha leaped up and bolted out of the house to meet Jesus before He reached their doorway.

But how did Martha's sister Mary respond? The ever-pensive Mary *stayed* in the house, *waiting* for the Savior. "Mary was sitting in the house" (John 11:20) until word arrived that "the Teacher has come and is calling for you" (verse 28).

Joining Jesus outside the town, dear Mary could only fall at His holy feet and declare her faith. "Lord," she cried, "if You had been here, my brother would not have died" (verse 32).

These sisters, this proverbial "odd couple," show us two ways of managing life. And please note, each way has its benefits. Martha definitely got things done and made things happen, but don't miss the importance of spending time in "the Mary mode," waiting on the Lord. When we choose to spend time out of sight and close to Jesus, important things can happen:

🎵 We read and study God's Word.

🎵 We linger in sweet prayer.

🎵 We commit to memory favorite Scriptures.

🎵 We meditate on things of the Lord.

In our busy world, we may be tempted to think that time alone with God, time spent waiting on the Lord, doesn't accomplish much. We may even think it's unimportant. After all, no one sees it, and there is no glory, no splash, no notice, nothing to measure or count. Yet time regularly spent with God bears fruit that can grow only in the shade of His presence. Consider these thought-provoking words of nineteenth-century Scottish lecturer Henry Drummond:

> *Talent develops itself in solitude;*
> *the talent of prayer, of faith,*
> *of meditation, of seeing the unseen.*[2]

Do you desire to bear this kind of heavenly fruit that grows only in the shade of God's presence? Then, today and every day, seek the solitude such divine fruit requires.

Two Faces of Love

Before we bid Mary and Martha Godspeed, let's peek through the window into their home one more time. The whole family is there—Mary, Martha, and, praise God, their brother, Lazarus, whom Jesus raised from the dead! We see a truly joyous celebration as these grateful folks prepare another meal for their beloved Jesus (John 12:2). The scene is both priceless and instructive.

We know that both Martha and Mary loved Jesus, but Martha showed her love for Him in practical matters and Mary in the pious. Please take these two images of two aspects of love along with you today...and every day...as you express to God your love for Him.

> *Service*—As usual, "Martha served" (verse 2). Are we surprised? No, service is Martha's way of expressing love! She was a practical woman, and hers was a practical love. She delighted in meeting the needs of the One she loved so dearly.

And you? Are you faithful to serve wherever God has placed you, remembering that whatever you do, you are to do heartily, "as to the Lord and not to men" (Colossians 3:23)? Do you regard the practical tasks at home—meals to prepare, floors to sweep, and clothes to wash—as ways of expressing your love for God as well as for others? While these daily duties may seem insignificant, God knows the sacrifice involved and is pleased when we serve as unto Him!

> *Worship*—And, as usual, Mary worshiped. Are we surprised? No, Mary was ever desirous of worshiping the Lord. On this particular evening, the grateful Mary chose to pour out her worship by pouring out expensive oil over Jesus' feet in an act of extravagant love. And then, as though that weren't enough, she "wiped His feet with her hair" (verse 3)!

Are you, fellow lover of the Lord, an uninhibited worshiper of God? Do you seek new ways to show your love for Him? Oh, your acts of adoration may be scoffed at, as were Mary's (verses 4-6). People may consider your sacrifices of worship unwise, wasteful, even foolish. But once again, God welcomes the gifts of worship you bring to pour out at His feet (verses 7-8). So make them lavish! And make them every day! Pour out your love in as many ways as you can…and as often and generously as you can!

~ Mary and Martha's Message for Your Life Today ~

As I wrote this chapter on the contrasting yet equally remarkable lives of these two sisters, I had difficulty naming their section. Should it be "Remarkable Friends"? Or should it be "Remarkable Love"? Or perhaps, it should be "Remarkable Worship"? Well, by now you know the answer—"Remarkable Love." But my dilemma points to the many wonderful messages these female siblings send our way. So take these many messages to heart.

- We must realize we can serve the Lord in different ways, whether in the tiny act of a meal prepared or the costly sacrifice of a lavish gift.

- We must watch out for busyness, making sure we are not too bothered and bogged down in the details of our work that we fail to worship the Lord.

- We must call upon Jesus as our first and primary source of strength when we face crises and tribulation.

Now, dear one, which message do you need to hear today?

Dorcas, Lydia, Priscilla, and Phoebe

~

Remarkable Servants

Selfless Service

She has "diligently followed every good work."
1 TIMOTHY 5:10

∿

*W*hat better way could we end a book about the remarkable women of the Bible than with a section on service, *selfless* service, *remarkable* selfless service? Delight yourself now in the exceptional lives of four women who show us how to serve one another in an exceptional manner.

Dorcas—The Eyes of Love

Let's first travel through the streets of Joppa, a city on the seacoast of the Mediterranean, and look in on a situation in the local church there. The Bible reports it this way: "At Joppa there was a certain disciple named Tabitha, which is translated Dorcas. This woman was full of good works and charitable deeds which she did" (Acts 9:36).

Serving in the congregation at Joppa was a lovely saint named Dorcas. In what ways did this woman minister to those in her church? She spent her hours and energy making coats and garments for the widows who were among the most needy persons in her day and culture. Dorcas didn't merely dream, make grand plans, or passionately desire to better the lives of her suffering sisters—she acted! We witness her working quietly, doing hands-on labor of love, putting forth practical efforts for the good of other people.

Dorcas—A Heart of Goodness

But then dear Dorcas died. And, oh, how the church mourned and grieved! Such a gracious, giving saint had been taken from them. As the church contemplated their loss, two of Christ's disciples from Dorcas' hometown went to the apostle Peter. They had heard that Peter had healed a paralyzed man in the nearby town of Lydda. Perhaps Peter could use this divine power on behalf of their Dorcas!

Upon hearing about Dorcas and her heart of goodness, Peter followed these men back to her crowded house where the widows of Joppa had assembled to show him the many clothes this thoughtful woman had made for them. Finally, after emptying the death chamber, Peter knelt, prayed, and commanded the corpse, "Arise." As the dead Dorcas began to stir, Peter helped her up. He then "presented her alive" to the saints and widows (Acts 9:41)!

Of course those in Joppa were thrilled! But other wonderful things resulted from the Lord's goodness:

> ♪ *God was glorified*—No person but God has the power to raise someone from the dead. Oh, how He must have been praised!

> ♪ *Faith was generated*—We are told that many believed as a result of Peter's miracle (verse 42). May God be praised for that too!

> ♪ *The people were gladdened*—Joy rippled through the church at Joppa. Dorcas was back! This loving, caring, generous woman who loved them—and God—was alive.

Now check *your* heart, dear one. Is yours a heart filled with God's love and goodness, a heart intent on doing good works for Him and His people? Do your lips overflow with praise for God's goodness? As the psalmist exhorts, "Give thanks to the LORD for His goodness, and for His wonderful works to the children of men!" (Psalm 107:8). Do so now!

Lydia—The Power of a Woman

"Never underestimate the power of a woman," the familiar cliché warns. In Lydia we certainly see the power of a woman when God chose to work through her! Consider some of the threads that made up the tapestry of Lydia's life.

She was a woman—This fact is important to her story. Why? Because ten men were required to organize a synagogue, and apparently this quorum was missing in Philippi. Therefore, the women met outside of town to pray (Acts 16:13). That's where we meet the remarkable woman Lydia.

She was a worshiper—Lydia believed in the God of Israel, but she had not yet become a follower of Jesus Christ.

She was attentive—One day, down by the riverside, the apostle Paul showed up at the women's prayer meeting, sat down, and began talking about Jesus...and Lydia listened.

She was baptized—As the truth about Jesus Christ penetrated Lydia's open heart, graciously and sovereignly "the Lord opened her heart to heed the things spoken by Paul" (Acts 16:14) and enabled her to receive the truth of salvation. The first thing Lydia did as a Christian, her first act of obedience and faithfulness to her Lord, was to be baptized.

She was influential—And Lydia wasn't baptized alone. Evidently she was instrumental in her entire household, relatives and servants alike becoming believers.

She was hospitable—Not only did Lydia open her heart, but she also opened her home. Paul's message had helped her, and now she wanted to help him and his friends by providing a home-away-from-home for them.

Lydia—The Purpose of Wealth

But there's more to Lydia's life—much more! Her story doesn't end with her baptism. She doesn't just drop off the pages of Scripture. No, two other threads are woven through the remarkable (and colorful!) life-weaving of Lydia.

She was a businesswoman—Lydia had lived in Thyatira, a city famous for its expensive purple dye. Now living in Philippi, Lydia sold clothes made from her deep-dyed purple fabrics. Because of the great cost of these goods, only the rich and the royal could afford them. As a dealer of these highly prized and costly garments, Lydia prospered.

She was generous—How did Lydia use her wealth? She cared for her relatives and household servants, but she also opened her home for the cause of Christ. Immediately after her conversion and baptism, she compelled Paul and his traveling companions to stay with her. And evidently her house was spacious because the budding church in Philippi met in Lydia's home (Acts 16:40).

There is nothing wrong or sinful with being successful in what you do. God blessed Lydia with ability, creativity, and a strong work ethic, just as He has other women who love Him. He undoubtedly expects us to live out our priorities (Titus 2:3-5), to work willingly with our hands (Proverbs 31:13), and to do whatever we do heartily and unto Him (Colossians 3:23). But with the blessings of ability and prosperity comes responsibility. To whom much is given, much is also required (Luke 12:48)! So we who love Him must always remember…

The source of wealth—We are not to think, "*My* power and the might of *my* hand have gained me this wealth." Instead we are to "remember the LORD your God, for it is *He* who gives you power to get wealth" (Deuteronomy 8:17-18)!

The purpose of wealth—We are "not to be haughty, nor to trust in uncertain riches but in the living God, who gives us richly all things to enjoy" and to "do good" so that we may be "rich in good works, ready to give, willing to share" (1 Timothy 6:17-18).

Priscilla—Bookends

Bookends. That image certainly comes to my mind as we look at both this next remarkable woman and her husband. Like a pair of bookends, they each held up their end as they served God's kingdom. Her name is Priscilla, and her mate-for-life was Aquila (Acts 18:2). Take a look at their twin traits.

Servants—Always mentioned together, Priscilla and Aquila stand as a team in both marriage and ministry.

Itinerants—Each time this dear couple is named, they're in a different location. They trekked from Rome...to Corinth...to Ephesus...and back again to Rome, and each city was a key site for ministry.

Industrious—Both husband and wife shared in their joint occupation of tentmaking and leatherworks.

Hospitable—This twosome opened up their "tent flaps" and took in the homeless apostle Paul (Acts 18:2). And here's another fact—the church in Ephesus met in their home (1 Corinthians 16:19).

Knowledgeable—With heartstrings tuned to God, Priscilla and Aquila listened attentively to Paul as he taught Jews and Greeks alike, gaining the knowledge they needed to serve Him in other places and other ways.

Willing—This husband–wife duo was willing to do anything and go anywhere, at any time and at any cost, for the cause of Christ. At one point, they even left Corinth with Paul to help him build up the body of Christ.

Perseverant—Expelled from Rome, this pair knew a life of persecution, yet they remained faithful to God. How? Let's learn a little more about Priscilla's sufferings.

Priscilla—Suffering and Glory

Our Priscilla probably came close to death as a martyr. She and her husband Aquila, somehow, at some time, intervened to save the apostle Paul's life. When he closed his letter to Rome, Paul wrote, "Greet Priscilla and Aquila...who risked their own necks for my life" (Romans 16:3-4). We have no details other than Paul's acknowledgment that they laid down their lives on his account. Literally, they had "placed their necks under the ax" for him.

While we may shudder to think of such a situation, the Bible is not shy about addressing the subject of persecution and suffering. Consider these two teachings.

Expect suffering—To live a godly life is to be a clear witness for the light of God's truth and love. Therefore, faithful believers must expect persecution and suffering in this dark and fallen world. In fact, Scripture promises "all who desire to live godly in Christ Jesus *will* suffer persecution" (2 Timothy 3:12). Another passage states, "For to you it has been granted on behalf of Christ, not only to believe in Him, but also to suffer for His sake" (Philippians 1:29).

Rejoice in suffering—Overflowing joy in Christ—whatever the current circumstances—is the reward of those who suffer for righteousness in this life. "Beloved, do not think it strange concerning the fiery trial which is to try you, as though some strange thing happened to you; but rejoice to the extent that you partake of Christ's sufferings, that when His glory is revealed, you may also be glad with exceeding joy" (1 Peter 4:12-13).

What awaits those of us who might meet a martyr's death like Priscilla faced? As one faithful saint loved to say, "It would be wonderful for a martyr to die with tears in his eyes, only to open his eyes and find the hand of the Lord Jesus wiping those tears away."[1] This joy and glory is the very *worst* that awaits God's faithful martyrs!

Phoebe—A Shining Servant

Dorcas. Lydia. Priscilla. What a variety of serving female saints! But we're not done yet! We can't leave this all-important quality without admiring yet another remarkable woman and servant. Her name is Phoebe, and she was God's gift to His faithful servant Paul. You see, Paul needed someone to help him. Let me explain.

Everyone needs help. If you're not sure of this truth, simply consider the challenges, stresses, and pressures of every day. Daily life brings with it much to do and many responsibilities to juggle, not to mention sorrows of heart to bear and physical ailments to cope with. Yes, everyone needs help! And the apostle Paul, God's choice servant, was no different. Second Corinthians 11 lists the many trials he faced, and in the face of those trials God gave Paul a servant to help him. Her name was Phoebe, meaning "bright and radiant," and Phoebe definitely stands as a bright and radiant example of the faithful servanthood God desires in each of His children—including us! Three special titles describe her shining faithfulness:

First, Paul calls Phoebe "our *sister*" (Romans 16:1). A devoted and committed member of the family of God, Phoebe was a Christian sister not only to Paul, but also to each and every saint in their fellowship.

Next the apostle commends Phoebe as "a *servant* of the church in Cenchrea" (verse 1). The honored title *servant,* from which our English words for *deacon* and *deaconess* come, denotes one who serves any and all in the church.

Finally Paul praises Phoebe as a *succorer:* "She has been a helper of many and of myself also" (verse 2). In classical Greek, *helper* refers to a trainer in the Olympic games who stood by the athletes to see that they were properly trained and rightly girded for competition. *Helper* literally means "one who stands by in case of need."

God's message to us is clear. As sisters who love God and whom He calls to love His people, we are to be in faithful attendance, to stand by in case of need, and then to willingly meet that need. Such dedicated, selfless service shines so brilliantly in our dark world!

(P.S. Like Paul, you too can thank God for such a servant as Phoebe, for she most likely delivered the priceless book of Romans to Rome for Paul. As one scholar has so aptly written, "Phoebe carried under the folds of her robe the whole future of Christian theology."[2])

Phoebe—Selfless Service

Someone quipped, "Some folks are poor spellers. They think *service* is spelled *serve us.*"[3] But that's certainly not the Bible's picture! As we've seen, God's Word shows us Phoebe, described by the apostle Paul as a sister, servant, and succorer. Before we end this book about God's remarkable servants, and before we leave Phoebe's bright and shining life of ministry, take to heart these thoughts about helping others.

Serve humbly—In the early church a servant and a helper was one who cared for the sick and the poor, ministered to martyrs and prisoners, and quietly assisted the people and ministry of the church whenever help was needed.

Serve always—Dear Phoebe's service seems constant. Hers was a long-distance track record of faithfulness. Probably a widow, she had served faithfully in the past and was still serving as she carried Paul's precious parchment letter from Corinth to Rome.

In summary, Phoebe was faithful to serve all, to serve humbly, and to serve continuously.

A Corps of Servants' Message for Your Life Today

Consider first the life-message of dear *Dorcas*, the woman with eyes—and a heart!—of love. Do you want your life to influence others for the Lord and touch them with His love? Then, as the Bible says, put on a heart of compassion and kindness (Colossians 3:12). Learn to look at people through Jesus' eyes of love and consider the afflictions and hardships you see. Then ask God, "What would better their condition? What can I do—big or small—to help?" When you, like Dorcas, work to meet the needs of others, your life will most definitely count for Christ!

Next evaluate the life of *Lydia* and her lessons to your heart. In what ways is your life similar to Lydia's? Are you worshiping regularly and being attentive to the teaching of God's Word? Have you been baptized according to the Lord's command to New Testament believers? Are you sharing with others the truth about salvation in Christ that you possess? And are you, like Lydia, opening your home and using your wealth to better the lives of the Lord's workers and His people? Remember, the power of a woman—even just one woman! It's truly remarkable!

Then there is *Priscilla's* remarkable life and example. If you are married, do you complement your husband's efforts? That's our calling, you know, whether or not our husbands are Christians (Ephesians 5:22; 1 Peter 3:1). As godly wives we are to support our husbands, dreams, hold up our end of the responsibility for family and home, and shoulder our part of the load of life. It takes both husband and wife—and the Lord's blessing!—to build a marriage and a family that glorify God. One more word: If you are single, remember that the pursuit of the godly qualities I've outlined is important for you, too!

And finally, there is *Phoebe*, sister, servant, and succorer. Do you offer the same heartfelt service to anyone and everyone, regardless of their stature? Are you happy to serve in the shadows when—and so that—others shine and the needs of people are met? Do you serve faithfully, quietly, and selflessly, seeking nothing for yourself, desiring no recognition, glory, or notice? And are you a servant not only in days gone by, but also in the present, and brimming with plans for serving in the future?

Dear fellow servant, our Jesus—the Son of Man who "did not come to be served, but to serve, and to give His life a ransom for many" (Matthew 20:28)—is the ultimate model for selfless service for those who love Him. Look to His example...and to Phoebe...and to Priscilla...and to Lydia...and to Dorcas...and follow in their faithful footsteps of selfless service!

Queens of Remarkable Faith and Grace

A Final Look

"Now faith is the substance of things hoped for,
the evidence of things not seen."
HEBREWS 11:1

In a country ruled by a king or queen, a royal crown is usually passed down from monarch to monarch. The crown—often magnificent, ornate, and bejeweled—serves as an emblem of the ruler's exalted position and title. But no position or title is more exalted or prestigious than "woman of faith," and through the ages many remarkable women who loved God have worn that crown—a crown of eternal righteousness.

Before we leave our survey of the remarkable lives of a sampling of such women of faith, look back again at these precious women who loved God and walked with Him—women who were honored to wear God's glorious crown of faith and grace. Gaze again at these women and their journey with God as recorded in God's permanent record book, the Bible.

- Eve fell in sin but went on to walk with God.

- Sarah followed where God led her husband.

- Rebekah prayed to God for a child.

- Jochebed defied the king and gave the world Moses.

- Miriam was a faithful sister and fellow leader of God's people.

- Rahab acted with faith, thereby accepting God's invitation to salvation.

- Deborah was a mother of Israel.

- Ruth and Naomi sought the best for each other and, in the end, were both blessed.

- Hannah cried out to God...and He answered her.

- Esther was the queen of courage.

- Elizabeth was righteous, even in the midst of trials.

- Mary was blessed among women, the mother of the Messiah.

- Mary and Martha loved Jesus in their own unique ways.

- Dorcas, Lydia, Priscilla, and Phoebe shone brilliantly in the shadows of humble service.

The Lord blessed each of these women and made her beautiful in His eyes. These beloved women endured times of hardship, adversity, deprivation, shame, and failure. All were called upon by God to make choices—hard choices, seemingly unbearable choices—by which they demonstrated their faith. Many showed their faith in God by a forward gaze—by a decision to not look backward at loss, at things forsaken, at failure, at mistreatment. Most chose to greet every sunrise with fresh hope rather than to stare backward at their sunsets of defeat or better days and become immobilized or embittered. Each endured, pressing on and drawing great strength from the Lord as she donned His crown of grace day by day, minute by minute, trial by trial.

Is your name among God's great women of faith through the ages? Are you actively looking to the Lord for His help, His wisdom, His enabling, and His grace? As one writer has remarked, "Our part is to trust Him fully, to obey Him implicitly, and to follow His instructions faithfully."[1] In doing so, my precious traveling companion, *you* live a remarkable life that points to the crowning, majestic beauty of faith and grace!

∾∾∾

A Prayer for a Remarkable Life

Lord, make of my life a pattern of remarkable accomplishment for the good of others and for Your glory. May I stand tall with these women of old and be a tribute to Your remarkable mercy and grace that is given to all those who call upon the name of the Lord. Amen.

∾∾∾

Notes

Chapter 1: Fairest of All Creation!

1. Nick Harrison and Steve Miller, *Survival Guide for New Dads* (Eugene, OR: Harvest House Publishers, 2003).

2. Herbert Lockyer, *All the Promises of the Bible* (Grand Rapids, MI: Zondervan Publishing House, 1962), p. 10.

Chapter 4: Rewards of Faith

1. A. Naismith, *A Treasury of Notes, Quotes & Anecdotes*, quoting May Gorrie (Grand Rapids, MI: Baker Book House, 1976), p. 246.

2. Donald Grey Barnhouse, *Let Me Illustrate* (Grand Rapids, MI: Fleming H. Revell, 1967), pp. 253-54.

Chapter 5: Ready, Willing, and Able!

1. Elisabeth Elliot, *Let Me Be a Woman* (Wheaton: IL: Tyndale House Publishers, Inc., 1977), p. 42.

Chapter 6: Tests of Faith

1. Herbert Lockyer, *The Women of the Bible* (Grand Rapids, MI: Fleming H. Revell, 1967), p. 137.

2. Drawn from *The Handbook of Bible Application*, Neil S. Wilson, ed. (Wheaton, IL: Tyndale House Publishers, Inc., 1992), p. 485.

Chapter 7: The Heart of a Mother

1. Herbert Lockyer, *The Women of the Bible* (Grand Rapids, MI: Fleming H. Revell, 1967), p. 79.

2. Horace Bushnell.

3. Phil Whisenhunt.

4. Stephen G. Green.

5. Ruth Vaughn.

Chapter 8: A Devoted Sister

1. Merrill C. Tenney, ed., *The Zondervan Pictorial Encyclopedia of the Bible*, vol. 4 (Grand Rapids, MI: Zondervan Publishing House, 1975), p. 875.

2. Miriam, Exodus 15:20. Deborah, Judges 4:4. Huldah, 2 Kings 22:14. Anna, Luke 2:36. Philip's four daughters, Acts 21:9.

3. Drawn from principles found in J. Oswald Sanders, *Spiritual Leadership* (Chicago: Moody Press, 1967).

Chapter 9: A Devoted Saint

1. Charles W. Landon.

2. Herbert Lockyer, *The Women of the Bible* (Grand Rapids, MI: Zondervan Publishing House, 1975), p. 113.

3. "Elisabeth Elliot Leitch: Held by God's Sovereignty," *Worldwide Challenge*, January 1978, pp. 39-40.

4. M.R. DeHaan and Henry G. Bosch, *Bread for Each Day* (Grand Rapids, MI: Zondervan Publishing House, 1962), June 23.

Chapter 10: A Cameo of Courage

1. John Oxenham, "The Ways," as quoted in James Dalton Morrison, ed., *Masterpieces of Religious Verse* (New York: Harper & Brothers Publishers, 1948), #936.

Chapter 11: A Portrait of Transformation

1. Author unknown.

2. Samuel Johnson.

3. Hebrews 11:11,23,31.

Chapter 13: Enduring Difficult Times

1. Matthew Henry, *Matthew Henry Commentary*, vol. 2 (Peabody, MA: Hendrickson Publishers, 1991), pp. 204-05.

2. William O. Cushing, circa 1896.

Chapter 14: Enjoying God's Blessings

1. John MacArthur, *The MacArthur Study Bible* (Nashville: Word Publishing, 1997), p. 373.

2. Jim George, *A Man After God's Own Heart* (Eugene, OR: Harvest House Publishers, 2002), p. 148.

3. Herbert Lockyer, *The Women of the Bible* (Grand Rapids, MI: Zondervan Publishing House, 1975), pp. 144-49.

Chapter 15: A Weaving of Grace

1. Herbert Lockyer, *Dark Threads the Weaver Needs* (Old Tappan, NJ: Fleming H. Revell Company, 1979).

2. William Temple, Archbishop of Canterbury.

3. James Strong, *Strong's Exhaustive Concordance of the Bible* (Nashville: Abingdon Press, 1973), p. 95.

Chapter 16: Threads of Sacrifice

1. Ray Beeson and Ranelda Mack Hunsicker, *The Hidden Price of Greatness* (Wheaton, IL: Tyndale House Publishers, Inc., 1991).

2. Curtis Vaughan, gen. ed., *The Old Testament Books of Poetry from 26 Translations* (Grand Rapids, MI: Zondervan Bible Publishers, 1973), p. 578.

3. Henri Frederic Amiel.

4. John Mason.

5. Elisabeth Elliot, *The Shaping of a Christian Family* (Nashville: Abingdon Press, 1973), p. 95.

Chapter 17: The Beauty of Courage

1. Reverend E.H. Hamilton, China Inland Mission missionary.

2. Richard C. Halverson, "Perspective" newsletter, Oct. 6, 1977. (Gender changed.)

Chapter 18: Consecrated to God

1. Walter B. Knight, *Knight's Master Book of New Illustrations* (Grand Rapids, MI: Wm. B. Eerdmans Publishing Co., 1979), pp. 204-05.

Chapter 19: Highly Favored One

1. Herbert Lockyer, *The Women of the Bible* (Grand Rapids, MI: Zondervan Publishing House, 1975), p. 92.

2. J.A. Thompson, *Handbook of Life in Bible Times* (Downers Grove: IL: InterVarsity Press, 1986), pp. 83-85.

3. Drawn from Elizabeth George, *Loving God with All Your Mind* (Eugene, OR: Harvest House Publishers, 1994), p. 183.

Chapter 20: O Worship the King!

1. Walter B. Knight, *Knight's Master Book of New Illustrations* (Grand Rapids, MI: Wm. B. Eerdmans Publishing Company, 1979), pp. 204-05.

2. Ray and Anne Ortlund, *The Best Half of Life* (Glendale, CA: Regal Books, 1976), p. 79.

3. Walter B. Knight, *Knight's Master Book of New Illustrations*, pp. 204-05.

4. Gien Karssen, *Her Name Is Woman* (Colorado Springs: NavPress, 1975), p. 131.

5. Merrill F. Unger, *Unger's Bible Dictionary,* quoting Keil (Chicago: Moody Press, 1972), p. 1172.

Chapter 21: A Woman After God's Own Heart

1. *Life Application Bible* (Wheaton, IL: Tyndale House Publishers, Inc., and Youth for Christ, 1988), p. 1471.

Chapter 22: A Portrait of Devotion

1. German scholar Johann Albrecht Bengel.

Chapter 23: Two Faces of Love

1. Drawn from Elizabeth George, *A Woman's Walk with God* (Eugene, OR: Harvest House Publishers, 2000), pp. 67-70.

2. Henry Drummond, *The Greatest Thing in the World* (New York: Thomas Crowell & Co., n.d.), p. 22.

Chapter 24: Selfless Service

1. Dr. Louis Talbot from Carol Talbot, *For This I Was Born* (Chicago: Moody Press, 1977), p. 208.

2. Marvin R. Vincent, *Word Studies in the New Testament,* vol. III, *The Epistles of Paul,* quoting Renan (Grand Rapids, MI: Wm. B. Eerdmans Publishing Co., 1973), p. 177.

3. Robert C. Cunningham.

A Final Look

1. V. Raymond Edman.

Personal Notes

Personal Notes

Personal Notes

Personal Notes

Personal Notes

Personal Notes

Personal Notes

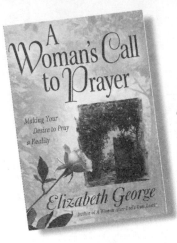

A Woman's Call to Prayer

Do you long for a meaningful prayer life but find that the demands of family, work, and home get in the way of your good intentions? Whether you're a prayer "wanna-be" who wonders how to take your first step into prayer or a seasoned prayer-warrior who aspires to continue in the battle, Elizabeth George will help you make your desire to pray a reality. You'll learn practical ways to—

✓ refresh your commitment to pray

✓ lift family and friends up to God

✓ discover God's will for your life

✓ worship God through prayer

Begin—or improve!—your journey of prayer. Elizabeth provides the inspiration, motivation, and step by step guidance you need to answer God's call to prayer.

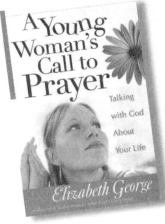

A Young Woman's Call to Prayer

Elizabeth George, author of *A Young Woman After God's Own Heart,* which reached #1 on Christian Marketplace's Young-Adult bestseller list, offers another exciting teen book—*A Young Woman's Call to Prayer.*

Elizabeth reveals the explosive power and impact of prayer on everyday life. Young women will discover how to establish a regular prayer time, pray for needs, and live God's will. Teens can experience enthusiastic prayer!

A Woman's Call to Prayer and *A Young Woman's Call to Prayer* are available at your local Christian bookstore or can be ordered from:

Jim and Elizabeth George Ministries
P.O. Box 2879 • Belfair, WA 98528

Toll-free fax/phone: 1-800-542-4611
www.ElizabethGeorge.com

If you've benefited from *The Remarkable Women of the Bible,* you'll want the complementary volume

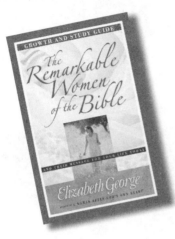

The *Remarkable Women* of the *Bible*

Growth and Study Guide

This guide offers thought-provoking questions, reflective studies, and personal applications that will enrich your life as you follow the examples of the remarkable women in Scripture.

This growth and study guide is perfect for both personal and group use.

The Remarkable Women of the Bible Growth and Study Guide is available at your local Christian bookstore or can be ordered from:

Elizabeth George
P.O. Box 2879
Belfair, WA 98528
Toll-free fax/phone: 1-800-542-4611
www.ElizabethGeorge.com

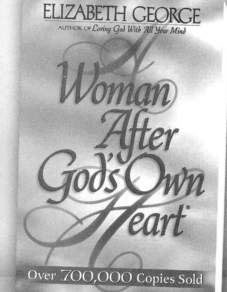

A Woman After God's Own Heart® Study Series

BIBLE STUDIES FOR BUSY WOMEN

"God wrote the Bible to change hearts and lives. Every study in this series is written with that in mind—and is specially focused on helping Christian women know how God desires for them to live."

—Elizabeth George

Sharing wisdom gleaned from more than 20 years as a women's Bible study teacher, Elizabeth has prepared insightful lessons that can be completed in 15 to 20 minutes per day. Each lesson includes thought-provoking questions and insights, Bible study tips, instructions for leading a discussion group, and a "heart response" section to make the Bible passage more personal.

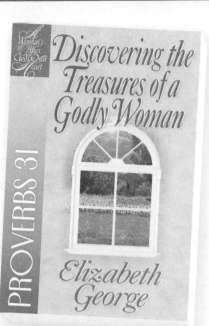

Proverbs 31 0-7369-0818-8

Philippians 0-7369-0289-9 | 1 Peter 0-7369-0290-2 | 1 Timothy 0-7369-0665-7 | Judges/Ruth 0-7369-0498-0

Esther 0-7369-0489-1 | James 0-7369-0490-5 | Life of Mary 0-7369-0300-3 | Life of Sarah 0-7369-0301-1

HARVEST HOUSE PUBLISHERS

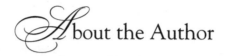# About the Author

Elizabeth George is a bestselling author and speaker whose passion is to teach the Bible in a way that changes women's lives. For information about Elizabeth's books or speaking ministry, to sign up for her mailings, or to share how God has used this book in your life, please write to Elizabeth at:

Elizabeth George
P.O. Box 2879
Belfair, WA 98528

Toll-free fax/phone: 1-800-542-4611
www.ElizabethGeorge.com

≈

Books by Elizabeth George

- Beautiful in God's Eyes
- Encouraging Words for a Woman After God's Own Heart®
- God's Wisdom for a Woman's Life
- Life Management for Busy Women
- Loving God with All Your Mind
- Powerful Promises for Every Woman
- The Remarkable Women of the Bible
- A Wife After God's Own Heart
- A Woman After God's Own Heart®
- A Woman After God's Own Heart® Deluxe Edition
- A Woman After God's Own Heart® Prayer Journal
- A Woman's Call to Prayer
- A Woman's High Calling
- A Woman's Walk with God
- A Young Woman After God's Own Heart
- A Young Woman's Call to Prayer

Children's Books

- God's Wisdom for Little Girls

Study Guides

- Beautiful in God's Eyes Growth & Study Guide
- God's Wisdom for a Woman's Life Growth & Study Guide
- Life Management for Busy Women Growth & Study Guide
- Loving God with All Your Mind Growth & Study Guide
- Powerful Promises for Every Woman Growth & Study Guide
- The Remarkable Women of the Bible Growth & Study Guide
- A Wife After God's Own Heart Growth & Study Guide
- A Woman After God's Own Heart® Growth & Study Guide
- A Woman's Call to Prayer Growth & Study Guide
- A Woman's High Calling Growth & Study Guide
- A Woman's Walk with God Growth & Study Guide

Books by Jim & Elizabeth George

- God Loves His Precious Children
- God's Wisdom for Little Boys
- Powerful Promises for Every Couple
- Powerful Promises for Every Couple Growth & Study Guide

Books by Jim George

- God's Man of Influence
- A Husband After God's Own Heart
- A Man After God's Own Heart
- A Young Man After God's Own Heart